Tell it to the Mafia

BY JOE DONATO

as told to Wyn Hope

Carol —

Lord Bless you
& Yours.

In Jesus Love

Br. Joe ✝

1

"Your Honor, we, the people of the State of California intend to ask the death penalty in the trial of Joseph Daniel Donato, accused of murder in the first degree."

A jolt went through me as I heard the words. This was no Cagney movie; this was *it*, and I had the lead role. I took a sidelong glance around the courtroom and noted with satisfaction that most of the eyes were on me. Murder One—the boys in the underworld would be watching this one, too. When you have blood on your hands and beat a murder rap, you're *something!* Even 'the moustaches,' the grizzled old Mafia chieftains, took notice and filed your name away for future reference.

Feigning shame, I lowered my eyes to my shoes—old, brown and scuffed, instead of the Italian leather beauties I was accustomed to. But Joey the Actor had to stay in character, and for the duration of the trial, I would wear the same clodhoppers and cheap wrinkled suit to

1

match. Once, as a boy, I had shined the shoes of some pretty big men in the underworld; now, I was wearing those shoes. Except for the trial, of course, but that wouldn't last long.

In 1940, in Reading, Pennsylvania, you got a nickel for a shoeshine. And for a ten-year-old kid at the lingering edge of the Depression, that was a lot. Reading was a slow, going-nowhere town to grow up in, even in the best of times. And I grew up there in the worst. I could never remember not being cold, except in the middle of the summer, and I was hungry almost all the time.

We were a big, poor, Italian family, in the middle of a run-down neighborhood full of big, poor families. My dad was on relief from the day I was born. A Calabrese from the toe of Italy, he could neither read nor write, and spoke only broken English, at best. As a result, the only work he could get, when work was available which it almost never was, was pick-and-shovel work, usually digging ditches for the WPA at twelve dollars a week. So we never really had quite enough clothes or food, or coal to heat the drafty old three-story brick barn we lived in.

I loved my dad. The youngest of five brothers, I would go with him to scrounge lumps of coal from the ash heaps outside the steel mills, with socks pulled over my hands, because we couldn't afford gloves. In the summer, I'd help him tend the garden in the backyard. Any vegetables we ate, we had to grow ourselves.

I loved my dad, but the feeling was not mutual. One day, I overheard him say to a visitor, as he pointed to one brother after another, "Now him, I like. And him, and him. Joey," he said, pausing as he came to me, "Joey, I don't like. But Tony I like, and Ralph—" Maybe it was because I was shorter and skinnier than my brother, and he thought of me as the runt of the litter, I didn't know. But I made up my mind that someday, somehow, I would be a big man in his eyes. And my own.

Not that our life together was unhappy. How can you be unhappy with seven brothers and two sisters around? Sleeping three in a bed, oftentimes we'd wake up and start roughhousing. But even when dad came up and laid into us with a rubber hose, we were taking our lumps together.

My mother was also hardworking. We had no carpets, but the bare wooden floors were kept scrubbed spotless. The greatest times were the Christmases when rich folks brought us baskets of food and sent us to the big stores to buy complete outfits of clothes.

Ours was a typical poor neighborhood. Many nationalities were there, with a fair sprinkling of blacks, and we all played together in the streets. There was no racial prejudice, though we often made fun of the odd Amish people who lived on neat farms in the nearby countryside.

From an early age, I was aware of the underworld. Their activities were wide open, but my parents and all the rest of the neighborhood just seemed to ignore it. All dad would say was, "If you live by the sword, you die by the sword." And whenever I'd get into trouble, he'd warn me, "You'd better straighten up!"

But the men of the underworld were my idols, from the time I'd shined their expensive shoes and seen the big rolls of fifty and hundred-dollar bills as they'd pay me and leave a large tip. They drove in big shiny cars and wore flashy clothes. I dreamed of being like that someday.

School didn't interest me much, though mom had had some schooling and was determined that we would have proper educations. The best memory from those early years was the realization that I had a special talent for entertaining. I found I could mimic my teachers and some of the movie stars I'd heard on the radio and seen in the movies. I had a chance to try out my routines at school assemblies.

3

"Rattlebones" was my nickname; I was only five-foot-six, a hundred and fifteen pounds. But I could not stand being treated as a little punk, and the moment anyone did it, I would go into a frenzy. My fights were always with bigger guys, and I would use any equalizer I could lay my hands on, sometimes using a club or knife to defend myself. My older brother, Tony, was always having to look out for me. By the time I was in eleventh grade, they gave up and threw me out of school as an incorrigible, which gave me a lot more time to devote to my favorite pastime—crime.

My activities outside the law had started in a small way when I was around eleven. Because of the hard times, the guys I ran with would steal milk from people's doorsteps, and I was right along with them. World War II had just begun, and so cigarettes were a rare luxury; we would steal them from the few stores that had them, then sell them. We'd steal anything, even air rifles, which we would stick down our pants legs, and then walk out stiff-legged like we were crippled. This invariably evoked sympathy from any store personnel who happened to notice us, and it struck them as curious that so many crippled kids the same age lived in the same town.

There were plenty of fights with kids from other neighborhoods, but our gang was close and loyal. We shared together—and ended up in Juvenile Court together. This happened over and over again. Our mothers would go to court with us, the Judge would give us a warning and let us go. And we'd go right on doing the same things.

One of our rackets was to strip parts off cars, and hardware from vacant houses, because the price of metals was high and we knew we could sell them with no questions asked. When we were caught, some of the guys weren't released but were sent to reform school. When they'd come out, they'd tell us about the terrible conditions—but also about the new tricks they learned

4

while in the school, making them better equipped for lives of crime.

When I was about thirteen, I began to notice girls. I met some from nice families, but the parents didn't want their daughters to associate with dagos. So mostly my girls were easy to pick up, and a few were so easy, we were among the first guys in the country to be treated for gonorrhea with a new wonder drug called penicillin. I met a lot of girls in the theaters. Our whole gang would get in by having one kid pay his admission, then sneak us in the side exit. I loved movies—especially the gangster films with Humphrey Bogart, James Cagney, and Edward G. Robinson.

I was a dreamer as I grew up. Often I'd dream I could fly, that if I'd run down the street and flap my arms, I could just soar up into the sky. It was a wonderful feeling. I'd look forward to going to sleep at night just to have that dream. But my greatest dream was to be a gangster, ride in a big car, wear expensive clothes, and have a pile of money to spend. I make up my mind then and there that I was never going to be poor.

Gambling was going on all around us. People bet on horses and played the numbers, and there were bookies all over the place. Even my buddies and I would pitch dimes against the line to see who'd win.

One of my pals was a real tough kid named Willie. He carried a switchblade knife and a pair of brass knuckles. I started carrying a knife, too. One day Willie had a fight with a boy and split his face open with the brass knuckles. With blood pouring down the corner of his cheek, the other kid pulled out his switchblade and stuck Willie in the side. Willie ran until he was too weak, then fell. Within a few days, he had died—by the sword that he had lived by. It should have been a warning to me, but this was the life I'd chosen, and the risk was part of what made it exciting.

One January day the gang stole a fourteen-foot rowboat, and I was, of course, all for trying it out as soon as possible, despite the fact that the Schuylkill River, which ran through the town, was high, cold, and at its most treacherous at this time of year.

The boat needed some fixing, but before long, it was ready. I ran home to get some boots, specifically my dad's hip-high waders, because I thought they most closely resembled the pirate boots I'd seen in the movies. I was on my way out the door with them when my mother happened to catch sight of me.

"Hey, Joe! Where do you think you're going in those?"

"Down to the river, mom. The boys have a boat, and—"

"You're not going in no boat in those boots. You tip over, they'll fill up, and you'll drown. You go get short boots."

"Aw, mom—"

"Do it." And I did. My mother stood for no backtalk. She'd take a broom handle to any one of us, and we'd rather be beaten by dad than her.

We river pirates launched the boat early in the afternoon and set off. As we got out in the middle of the rapids, things began to happen fast. The current was too much for us, and we were swept broadside into the trough of the waves, with the full force of the wind on the length of the boat.

The next thing we knew, the boat had capsized, and as my face hit the icy cold water, the thought went through my mind that this was the end. My hat, heavy jacket, and boots didn't help any, and in no time I was in trouble. Normally, I was a pretty fair swimmer, but with a mouthful of water and everything else, I was gripped by panic, which is like being half paralyzed. Somehow I managed to struggle to the surface and called out weakly for help.

The boat was gone, way downriver, and my two buddies had made it to shore. But they heard my cries, and

6

dived back in for me. I could feel myself getting weaker fast, but at the sight of them, new strength seemed to flow into me, and it was as if a big hand were underneath me, supporting me, like when a father first teaches his kid how to swim.

They reached me, though we were all carried a long ways downriver, and together we made it to the shore. We went to my house first, and I had no idea what mom would say. But when she took one look at us, she seemed to know what had happened, even before we could tell her. There was no hollering, no broom handle. She dried us off, then sat us down and fed us hot soup. And thanked God for saving us.

Church was not a part of our lives. Although I can still remember my mother praying, asking God to watch over us kids, she rarely went to Mass. The black kids attended church every Sunday, and I sort of admired them for this. So my brothers and I decided to begin going to the Catholic church. We sat for two and one-half hours listening to the priest talking in Latin. We couldn't understand a word of it and couldn't figure out why they were lighting all those candles. I came out of that church stiff from sitting so long and bored to death. My brothers agreed it was not for us, so we never returned. The priest was rather upset about it and talked it over with our parents, but dad said if we wanted to pray, we could do it at home.

By the time I was seventeen, my life had settled into a pattern of sorts. Going to baseball and football games, and other things that kids my age enjoyed, had no appeal for me; I considered them the pastimes of weak snobs. My time was spent working and stealing and running around with girls. I had a part-time job as a box-boy in a grocery store, a job I considered strictly temporary, and I idolized the Dead-End Kids and the East Side gang in the gangster movies. That was the way to live!

In fact, my whole world was a movieland fantasy, which I was able to reinforce through impersonations of my favorite stars—James Cagney, Edward G. Robinson, Al Jolson, Eddie Cantor. I had regular routines which I polished to perfection. People used to love them, and everyone would encourage me to go into show business, which sounded fine to me. But how?

The answer came in the form of a Horace Heidt amateur contest in our local movie theater, the Rajah. I entered, I was really *on*, and I won. And it was beautiful—all that applause. For me. Even so, that probably would have been the end of it, had it not been for Bernie Kenney, the Rajah's owner. Bernie was convinced that my talent was going to take me right to the top, and he started acting as my manager. The first thing I knew, he had me booked into a big hotel in Atlantic City, and from there I went to the Adams Theatre in Newark, where I appeared with some of the top name bands. I even emceed one show, on the billing of which were the Three Stooges.

When I came back to Reading, my chest was out six inches in front of me with pride. If I had been insufferably cocky before, now I was impossible. Bernie put me in some more shows at the Rajah, and then he took me to Elmira, New York, where I was in a contest with a ten-year-old saxophone player named Kennie Blakecki. That contest was especially important because it was going to be broadcast over the radio.

As luck would have it, I had to go first, which meant that the saxophone player would be fresher in the audience's memory when it came time for them to applaud for their favorite. I had to be good, and I was, but that little kid was something else on the saxophone. When he got done, we both stood in the wings while the audience voted.

"Joe Donato!" the emcee cried, and I held my breath as the needle on the electric applause meter swung far over to the right.

"Kennie Blakecki!" Incredibly, the needle swung wide again. I was sure it hadn't swung quite as far for him as it had for me, and I was turning to offer my condolences to Kennie when I heard the emcee say, "Folks, it's so close we're going to have to vote again! Get ready now—"

Vote again? What's he talking about, vote again? Anybody who could see his way into the theater could see that the needle hadn't swung quite as far the second time. Why, the—

"Joe Donato!" Again the needle swung, as far as the first time. Okay, that should settle it.

"Kennie Blakecki!" Listen to those people beating their palms! What are they trying to do? The needle swung as far as before and held there for a moment before falling back.

"The winner," and the emcee paused for maximum effect, "Kennie Blakecki!" *What?* You've got to be kidding! What kind of an angle was that emcee reading the meter on, anyway? Why, of all the—and all the way home in Bernie's car I refused to be consoled, grousing about the cruelty of my fate. If I had believed in God, I would have been convinced He had it in for me.

But nothing could have been further from the truth. The winner of that contest was to return to Elmira the next week to defend his championship. Kennie, his mother, a guitar player, and my friend Bernie all went together in a private chartered plane. Coming back to Reading, the plane crashed, and the pilot, Bernie, and Kennie's mother were killed.

It took me a year to get over Bernie's death, and each time I thought of it, I was reminded that the first contest I had lost, I'd actually won. First the boat accident, then the plane crash. . . . It was almost as if I was living a charmed life.

I'd always had a violent temper, and I admit I didn't

try very hard to control it. In the summer of 1947, I had trouble with a man named John Habecker. He was about twenty-two. During our argument, he grabbed me and started to choke me. Enraged, I ran home and got a gun I'd made from a rifle and waited for him outside our favorite pool hall. Finally, he showed up, and when he came close, I put the gun right in his face. I wanted to scare him, and I did; he turned white as a sheet.

Then things started to happen: someone called the police, and in no time there were four squad cars there. When they took the gun from me, they found it was loaded. So—off to jail to await trial. I pleaded guilty and was sentenced to from two months to one year in the Berks County Prison. (Fifteen years later, John Habecker, the man I'd threatened, became Chief of Detectives in my hometown.)

I took my first stretch of prison life in good stride. After all, if I behaved myself, I would be out in two months. I was soon entertaining my fellow prisoners by doing imitations of movie stars. I had quite a routine by then: George Burns, President Roosevelt, Jimmy Durante, Jack Benny, Amos 'n' Andy, and many others. Everybody got a big kick out of my performances—prisoners and guards alike. The warden and the guards were pretty nice guys. As a matter of fact, they went overboard to help many of the prisoners.

As I got acquainted with the prisoners and I listened to their talk, I realized they were all born losers, but they had one thing in common: they were all prison lawyers. They knew all the answers and were eager to give you advice on how to beat the rap.

I was out of prison in sixty days. Some of the boys were waiting for me with a classy-looking girl and a car. That night, the two of us celebrated with a real wild party.

As time went on, the old gang broke up; guys got married and found new circles of friends. I went from one job to another—for a while in a store, then on a railroad, and finally in a hospital. The best part of that job was getting to put on shows for the patients. I added more voices to my act, and the hospital staff told me how great I was, that I should be in show business. But being a star never had as great an appeal as being a kingpin in the underworld.

One night in 1951, I got into a dice game and was lucky. By the time I left, I had enough money for a bus ticket to California. That was where I'd always wanted to go. Sunny California, where the gold was lying in the streets! I took a bus to Los Angeles, and hunted up my brother who was a bartender. For about two months, I tended bar with him. I was scared and lonely in the big city, but I had arrived in the Land of Opportunity, and I was determined to make it big.

2

I hadn't been in Los Angeles long before I met Tommy, a slick operator. He got me a job in a gyp joint on Main Street. In front of the bar would be five or six sexy girls, wise to the ways of enticing men into the place. There was a set routine: as bartender, I'd give a girl a double shot of cheap wine and charge the man $2.50 for it. Then I'd give her a coke in another glass. She'd pretend to drink the double shot but, instead, would spit it into the coke.

In the meantime, I'd see to it that the man's drink was well spiked with vodka. Before long, he'd get so sick and dizzy he wouldn't know what he was doing, and it would be easy for the girl to steal his wallet. We kept a club behind the bar in case we needed to straighten out some of the guys. Many of the patrons got awfully mad—and who could blame them? But if they got too riled up and noisy, we'd call the police to haul them out of the joint.

One day I read in the paper that "Ted Mack's Amateur

Hour" was going to have a contest in Los Angeles. I decided to enter with my impersonations.

The show was held at the Shrine Auditorium and was broadcast on radio. I performed before a large audience, cocksure as I did my best. And it turned out to be the best; I won the contest, and was flown to New York for another competition. That was the first time I'd been on a plane, and remembering Bernie dying in a plane crash on the way back from that talent contest in Elmira, I was pretty nervous. We took off okay, but then I looked out the window into the darkness and saw fire coming out of the engines. I thought, "My God! This plane is going down! It's on fire!" It was a nightmare—all night. But we arrived safely.

The second contest was at the Vanderbilt Theatre—this time aired on radio and television. Again I came out on top, the winner in New York City, and they sent me to compete at Des Moines, Iowa, where I finally lost. From then on, I consciously turned my back on being a performer and earning an honest living. Returning to Los Angeles, I was asked to go to Las Vegas for interviews and to some of the top spots in California for auditions. Other performers would have given their right arms for the chances I was offered at that time. But instead of following the agents' advice, I found myself back in the Crown Hill area of Los Angeles with my old pal Tommy.

There I met Sol, a bookie. He took an interest in me and offered me a job taking bets for him on the phone. At last I was really "in!" In my spare time, I hung around the card room watching the men gamble. They'd bet $100 to $500 on one game of cards. I'd watch them shoot dice where there was from $8,000 to $50,000 in one game. This was more like it. I was getting close to real money.

Marijuana, back then, was not nearly as common as it is today, but it was the thing to do to be part of the crowd.

When we'd get together, we'd have our marijuana, plenty of good wine and food, and just relax. I should say that the weed didn't really relax you, it deadened you. I'd have a feeling of peace because my brain was numb. Driving my car after smoking marijuana, I'd feel I was on an ocean liner gliding along the highway. My reactions were so slow that time meant nothing.

I noticed changes in my speech, too. I'd repeat things, have trouble making sense, talk in a slurred, uneven way. For some reason, my appetite was tremendous, especially for sweets. I could eat a half gallon of chocolate ice cream in one sitting. I'd be so relaxed and confused, I'd sit and eat and eat and not realize it. It was the same with sex, too. I had this insatiable appetite and lost all sense of time.

One day when I was high on the weed, I made a mistake on the phone that cost Sol $1,600. He didn't realize that I was turned on, but he transferred me to a card club called the Taxi Drivers' Social Club. I was the bookie, taking bets, calling them in on the phone. We had some of the greatest, fastest gamblers in Los Angeles coming in there, and most of them bet heavily on the horses.

One of the bosses, called "The Bug," had been paying off some cops as protection. One day, he got involved in a card game. The policemen were waiting in the back alley for their payoff, but The Bug didn't bother to give them their hush money. They were plenty burned up, so in the next couple of days, we were rousted about every fifteen minutes. I was taken to jail, but because they had no evidence, I was released.

It was at this time I met Janie, a beautiful blue-eyed blonde. She was only seventeen and still in high school when we started dating—a really good person, naive and trusting. We were madly in love. I don't believe she realized how involved I was in illegal activities. Besides my bookmaking, I had connections with prostitutes and could make arrangements for abortions in California and

14

Mexico. I couldn't help but feel sorry for women who didn't want to be pregnant and waited so long they were desperate.

But I saw the sordid side of it, too. In fact, one of my buddies took his wife for an abortion in Mexico and lost her through a crude, messy job. For that reason, I would never take any cut from the doctors. I didn't want blood money. I had enough illegal activities to keep me busy and full of excitement. I was really rolling along high and was on my way to the top.

One day a letter from Uncle Sam arrived, bringing the grim news that I had been drafted. I told my buddies that somehow I'd be out in sixty days.

I was sent to Fort Mead, Maryland. When they looked at my record, they noted I'd been in some shows, so it was suggested I go into Special Services, entertaining troops. Here was another golden opportunity. But instead of taking their suggestion, I went AWOL for three days and landed in the stockade when I came back. I was soon in training again, and it really went against my grain. So eager was I to get back to the old life and Janie, that I decided to make like I was crazy. I knew I had the acting ability to put it across. One day in the barracks, after a fight with one of the guys, I grabbed a bayonet and started swinging at everyone in sight. All the guys scattered, and soon the place was full of MPs. They hauled me away in an ambulance to the hospital. It had worked! They gave me a Section 8, a medical discharge—within sixty days.

Back in Los Angeles, Janie was waiting for me. It was evident she was carrying my baby, so we went to a justice of the peace and got married, to give the child a name.

With my new responsibilities, I decided I'd better go legit, so I worked in the aircraft industry for a while, determined to go straight and be a good husband. I even gave up the marijuana bit for a while. But the aircraft industry was on hard times, and I was let out. Next, I got a job in a supermarket, but this was not at all what I'd wanted out of life. Janie and I began to argue and fight, and finally, I left her. I couldn't face the responsibilities of being a husband and father. I didn't care what happened to Janie or our baby that was due in only a month. All I cared about was me.

I took off for Lake Tahoe. It had always sounded glamorous, and I knew there was gambling there. Besides working as a waiter at night, I'd put on a couple of shows. The money was good, and I should have been happy there, but there was something hollow inside me. After six or eight months, I returned to Janie. She had given birth to a baby girl—a lovely child I was not to watch grow up, for after another argument I walked out on Janie forever.

I wanted to get Los Angeles, Janie, and the rackets out of my system, so I returned to my old hometown, Reading. For more than a year, I knocked around there. A divorce freed me from wife and child and pressures. My parents were glad to have me near again, but they were not so happy as I slid back into my old habits and troubles.

One night, I was walking down the street with a girl when we were approached by a man and two women. As they passed, they said something smart to my girl. An argument followed, and in uncontrollable fury, I banged the man's head against an iron fence. One of his women kicked me, and I hit her right back on the chin. I really wasn't too surprised when the cops came to the house the next day, charging me with assault and battery and aggravated assault and battery. I went to jail for one day and wound up paying a fine.

After that incident, I figured I might as well go back to Los Angeles. I found that Janie and the baby had left town. I couldn't blame her for trying to get our daughter away from such an irresponsible father.

I was soon back in the swing of things. My bookie job was waiting for me, and I also became more involved with prostitutes and marijuana. I had as many women as I wanted. One girl I remember was named Lorrie. She was beautiful enough to have been in the movies, but she was just another one of the hundreds of girls who come out to Hollywood, trying to be discovered. They use up all their money, then drift into prostitution. Like so many others, Lorrie began with marijuana and was finally hooked on heroin.

She lived with a guy named Pete, who loved to throw parties. Pete was a great cook and often turned out a delicious feast for as many as twenty people. I remember him always with a big cigar in his mouth. Many of our friends, some of the top men in the underworld, enjoyed getting in their kitchens and cooking their favorite meals. We'd all get full of wine, eat the fine food, then relax. Another friend was Whitie, a bookie. Often we'd go to his house, get stoned on marijuana, then have our wine and loads of food.

We had quite an active "social life" among us, and at these parties I met many professional shoplifters and burglars. I made a connection to buy hot merchandise, and soon learned one could buy anything from diamonds to TV sets. In fact, these thieves would often "take orders" for certain items before they'd lift them. Most of the shoplifting was from high-class stores. Nearly all those involved were on narcotics and had to steal to support the habit. All of a sudden, they'd disappear for six months or a year, and I'd know they'd been jailed on narcotics charges. After their release, they'd go back to their same habits until they were picked up again. They always looked like pictures of death, and they'd sell their souls for a fix. I had gotten so I didn't trust anyone I knew, and that was particularly true of those on heroin.

One warm summer night, I'd come out of the pool hall to get some fresh air and to take a break, when I saw this

17

cute-looking girl coming across the street. Eyeing her from stem to stern as was my custom, I noted that she was clean-cut and wore almost no make-up—not at all like the sort of girl one saw around that neighborhood, or that I was used to running with.

Crossing the street, she walked into the liquor store next to the pool hall, but I figured she wasn't going there for a bottle of booze. Sure enough, as I watched through the window, she bought a quart of milk. Back in those days, liquor stores doubled as delis, and you could buy almost anything there in the evening.

When she came out, I went up to her, bold as brass, and said, "Hey, I think you're cute, you know that? You're not from around here are you?"

That kind of direct approach usually elicited one of two responses. Fortunately, she was innocent enough to answer honestly, "I just moved in to live with my grand-mother down the block."

Up close, I noted that her eyes were green, and with her long, wavy, dark brown hair, she was real easy on the eyes. I promptly asked her for her telephone number, which, to my surprise, she gave to me. But I soon found out that Jean was no pushover; in fact, she was entirely different from the girls I usually took out. Our dates to-gether consisted of having a Coke, or going to the beach or playing Ping-Pong—and I loved it! This was the girl for me, the first I'd ever met that I'd want to take home to mom, and the first mom would ever have wanted to meet.

Jean was nineteen when we met, and she worked as a secretary. When she asked me what my work was, I thought for a moment, and then solemnly told her that I was an "agent." So confidential was I when I said it, that her eyes widened, and she never asked what organiza-tion I was an agent for, the FBI, the CIA, the Treasury Department, or what.

What's more, when I took her to the homes of my

underworld friends for dinner, I tipped them off in advance, and they were "agents," too. Jean never raised an eyebrow that no one ever asked how business was or mentioned how things were going in the office, and that all my friends seemed to do was cook big meals and have a good time. Colorful characters, these secret agents!

After a while, I sort of regretted the deception, but it had been going on too long to stop, and it really was an awfully good joke. Every so often, one of my friends would make a verbal slip and then back-pedal furiously to cover his error, while the rest of us bit our tongues to keep from laughing out loud.

In the meantime, Jean and I fell deeply in love and planned to be married. Nor were the plans upset when Jean's grandmother blew my cover. She used to play the horses a bit from time to time herself, and would send the odd bet over to the pool hall. Inevitably, she put two and two together. "Jean, honey, your Joe is no secret agent, unless it's for Hialeah and Pimlico. He's Little-Joe the Bookie!"

By that time it was too late. Maybe Jean thought that the love of a good woman could straighten me out. Anyway, we got married and left for Lake Tahoe and a wonderful honeymoon.

My wife continued to work at her secretarial job after our marriage, and I kept busy at my racket. About this time, I met Charlie. He was with the syndicate in Cleveland and had come out to Los Angeles with $100,000 in cash. Charlie was in with the people I worked for. He would be on the phones in our headquarters, and I'd work the card club and call in bets from the different gamblers. He'd take the bets, then call the race results to me later. We did this all day long.

I liked Charlie. To me, he was a prince of a guy. But he had one hang-up: he was never sober for more than two weeks at a time, and when he was drunk, he wasn't worth the room he took up. Between his drinking and gambling, his money didn't last long. He finally bought a bar, which hardly helped his alcohol problem. One day, very drunk, he accidentally hit his head on a lead pipe and was knocked out. Everyone thought he was just stiff from liquor, so they picked him up and put him on a couch. He lay there for two days before finally someone took a good look at him and discovered he was dead. Charlie left a very nice wife and family who gave him a big funeral where his underworld pals gathered to pay their last respects.

Gradually, I was learning all the tricks from the professional gamblers and thieves who hung around the card room. I knew every way to cheat with crooked dice and card games. We had all the top gamblers and underworld people coming to our place, because this was where the action was. They'd gamble at the drop of a hat. It was a melting pot for thieves, and I learned fast from all these underworld characters.

One of the gang was Angelo, a professional holdup man. He was a regular Samson—a rough, tough, ruthless guy. At one time, he had a crew of four or five men back East working with him. They'd hold up large gambling places. During one of their jobs back there, two of his friends were killed. Angelo was shot in the arm and another man was shot in the stomach. Angelo confided in me all his involvements in crime, even mentioning people who had had to be killed.

Working with him back East was Louie, as well-known as Angelo all over the country. These partners had the reputation of being the best in the business as far as safe-cracking, counterfeiting, and big holdups were concerned. Louie had been caught after he'd held up a bank messenger for $75,000. His love for big spending was his undoing. The FBI caught up with him, and he was convicted. Louie was now serving time in prison, but his sentence would soon be up.

Angelo and I decided to branch out and open up our

own bookie operation. We soon had a good thing going for us. We had bookmaking, gambling, con games—and dealt in hot merchandise, anything we could to turn a fast buck. We were a good combination. I was devoted to the business, though I myself didn't gamble. I'd only get into a game when I had the edge, only if I could cheat.

Although Angelo was a big shot in the underworld, he was a very unhappy man. He and his wife fought constantly, and both of them seemed to be miserable all the time. He was a man full of hate, and he didn't trust anyone. The nearest thing he had to religion was a belief in reincarnation. He thought he was going to come back as a bird.

Angelo's dad had become a Christian in his later years, and it was quite a joke to his son. It seems his dad had been severely crippled—hardly able to walk—due to a bad back. Then some Christians came to see him and offer prayers for his healing. When he recovered, he was so touched, he joined the Pentecostal Church and spent hours passing out tracts to win other souls. Angelo told me, "Can you imagine? My old man says he can't wait to die and go to heaven!" And we held our sides laughing.

3

Two years after our marriage, Jean gave birth to a baby girl. We named her Karen Lynne. Since Angelo was my closest pal, I decided to make him Karen's godfather. By this time, he and I were real pals. He liked to keep in shape, and we'd often play handball together at the YMCA. In our business, you need a certain amount of exercise to cope with the tensions.

Angelo and I had a good business together with about fifty people working for us. We kept everybody in line. Often he would get real violent when things didn't go to suit him. I remember one occasion in particular. He got so angry at our friend Tommy that he took a knife and cut his face. And I've seen him work over a guy by booting his face with his shoe.

Angelo taught me well. I was beginning to hate everyone, too. But inside me was a hollow, empty feeling I was to sense more and more. I started to neglect my family, curse my wife, scream whenever the baby made a noise, and I couldn't sleep at night. I really was a bundle of nerves, and nothing seemed to calm me down, not even the tranquilizers I started to take heavily. I had a secret fear of Angelo, knowing his hate and temper. One time, when he phoned and wanted to see me, I met him with a gun in each of my pockets. Because we were so closely involved in our business, I didn't want to cross him. That time, our argument was settled without any trouble, and I felt lucky, for Angelo would just as soon kill you as look at you.

Angelo kept telling me that when his pal Louie got out of jail and came West, they'd take over the town. This friend of his had once been sentenced to the electric chair for killing a man, then got a stay of execution at the last minute. He could kill a guy without batting an eye. Through Angelo, I got acquainted with most of the notorious members of the underworld.

We had the usual troubles in our personal relationships. Some of the people who worked with us were heavy drinkers and gambled a lot. When the time came to collect our money, they'd put us off with excuses. But they would finally pay up. They knew they'd better, or else they'd be in real trouble.

One day I had to take over the telephone in a bookie office. I hadn't been there long before the door flew open and in walked five big policemen, including one Officer Colmbs. Some time after my arrest, I learned he'd been following me. The cops knew our gambling and bookmaking operation was getting big in Los Angeles. Colmbs had had me under surveillance for weeks and that day tracked me to this bookie office. I was charged with three counts of bookmaking, but released on bail to await trial.

All this made Angelo meaner than ever. I don't believe I've ever known an unhappier, more unpredictably volatile man. I realized that a lot of his viciousness was due to the continual battling with his wife. He took his anger

23

out on everyone around him. Angelo's wife wouldn't complain quite as much at Angelo's going out if he was with me, so he was always trying to get me to go out with him, to a party, to play cards, and the like. But I had a new house, and I enjoyed working around fixing it up. So he would come over, whenever he felt like it, and make himself at home.

After a while, it got so he was telling me how to run my home, which I didn't appreciate, especially since he wasn't exactly making a success of running his own. One evening he came in as we were sitting at the kitchen table for dinner. Angelo joined us at the table, pulled out his knife, and started cleaning his fingernails.

It made me sick to watch him—and to realize that I was too afraid of him to say anything. But finally, it was so bad I didn't care, and I asked him if he wouldn't mind stopping—at least until we had finished eating. He ignored me, finished his nails, then put his knife away and left.

I was shaking with rage and frustration. I knew that if I ever crossed Angelo's will, he would kill me. It was harder than ever to get to sleep after that, and the nightmares were the worst I'd ever known.

I was getting meaner and meaner all the time. I stayed away from home a great deal, running around with a lot of different girls—wining and dining and living it up. My wife knew what was going on and complained to me that I was neglecting my family. When she'd open her mouth, I'd give her a smart slap and yell at her in the foulest language.

One morning after a particularly bad night, I was awakened by the phone. It was Angelo's wife, and she wanted me to run her downtown to pick up her unemployment check, which in itself was a joke. Groggy with sleep, I told her I was sorry, but I couldn't, and started to hang up.

"What do you mean telling me you can't? Who do

you think you're talking to, Mr. Joe Donato?"

"I know who I'm talking to, and I'm telling you that I don't feel well, and I'm not—"

"When Angelo hears about this, you're going to be one very unhappy little—"

"Well, you just tell Angelo whatever you damned well please!" I shouted, banging the receiver down. I was angry, but I was also scared. The fat was in the fire now.

Sure enough, less than an hour later, the phone rang again. Even before I picked it up, I knew. I was so scared I couldn't breathe, and an icy hand gripped my stomach. "Hello," I said, the receiver trembling in my hand.

"Joe! My wife tells me you just gave her a big beef on the phone, a lotta lip." It was Angelo, all right, and his wife had obviously distorted what had happened out of all proportion. I could just see her standing behind him, her arms folded on her chest, smiling with satisfaction.

"Angelo, that's not true," I said as calmly as I could. "She called me and asked me to run her—"

"Joe! Are you calling my wife a liar?"

"I'm just trying to tell you what happened." I could hear her now, on the other end of the phone, putting it to Angelo.

"I'm not going to let you talk about my wife that way! I'm going to come over there and—"

"No, you're not going to do anything, Angelo," I said, completely losing my cool. "I've had it with you coming around here whenever you damned well feel like it, trying to boss me around. From now on, you just stay the hell out of my house."

"Why, you lousy little punk!" He was screaming now. "You're nothing! Do you hear me, you're nothing! I'm gonna—"

"Do whatever you want, Angelo!" I shouted back, as mad as he was. "Take your best shot."

He slammed down the phone.

I was so scared, I felt like throwing up, but I had to

protect myself. The first thing I did was to get out my 30-06 deer-hunting rifle, the rifle with which I had covered many underworld conferences in the past. Angelo would be in a restaurant, meeting with some other racketeers to discuss territories and the like, and unbeknownst to them, I'd be across the street in a parked car, watching through the window, with the cross-hairs of my telescopic sight settled on the chest of their leader —just in case.

It was hardly the most wieldy or inconspicuous weapon I could have chosen with which to defend myself, but I wasn't thinking very clearly. I took it into the bathroom with me while I shaved, but I was kidding myself—the razor was jumping in my hand so bad that I could have cut my face in six different places. And that made me think of Angelo cutting up Tommy's face—

The doorbell rang, and everything drained out of me. All at once, I was glad it was going to happen this way, instead of in some dark alley. I could never have slept again, in any event.

Jean let him in, and he came straight back to the bathroom and opened the door.

"What are you doing? Shaving?" he said quietly, looking at the lather on my face.

"Yeah, I'm shaving," I said, equally quietly. There was a silence, and we looked at each other. Each saw in the other's eyes that there would be no backing down.

I took the rifle from behind the door and, holding it easily at my waist, pointed it in his direction. "Okay, Angelo, now just march right on out of here."

Angelo looked at the muzzle of the rifle and looked at me and burst out yelling.

"Yell all you want, Angelo!" I yelled back to make myself heard. "But just keep backing up! You don't scare me!" Inside I was shaking like a leaf.

"You little punk, don't you understand you're nothing?" His face contorted with disgust. I had had more than enough of his contempt.

26

"You try anything, and they'll carry you out of here! I'm not afraid of you—you hear me?—I'm not afraid of you!" But we both knew I was lying.

As I edged Angelo into the living room, Jean grabbed Karen, ran into the back bedroom, and slammed the door. Angelo's eyes were bulging in fury, and his cries sounded like those of a wild beast.

All of a sudden, there was a deafening explosion—then total silence. Angelo and I looked at each other, our mouths open in surprise. There was a small rod hole in the middle of his chest. He stood stock still, then took a half-step forward and fell to the floor, an end table and lamp going with him.

My wife came running out of the bedroom with Karen, and looked down at Angelo, her eyes widening in horror. She opened her mouth to scream, but nothing came out. She looked at me holding the rifle, and then turned and ran with Karen out the back of the house.

I let go of the rifle. It clattered to the floor, the noise of it startling me back to my senses. Always in the past, my last security was in my ability to think fast. And my ability to make the right snap decision had saved my life many times over; in fact, it (I thought) was the only thing which had kept me from going the way of so many of my late friends.

Joe! Joe! Joe! I yelled at myself. You got to start *thinking!* Get that mind in gear, fast! What first? Report it to the police. But don't call them direct, have the operator do it. You're too shook up to look up the number and dial it yourself. "O" is all you can manage. And have her call an ambulance, too, as if you didn't know that he was dying or already dead, and you wanted to save him.

I looked down at Angelo, and shook my head. His whole chest was drenched in blood—and he wasn't moving. I ran to the phone, got the operator, and told her everything.

27

Then I went out front to wait for the police and wave them to the right house. I was going to be the perfect picture of distraught cooperation. Within three minutes, the first patrol car came careening around the corner. I waved to them and reached behind me to open the front door and show them in. But the door wouldn't open.

Oh, my God, the latch had been on when I shut it! I panicked then. How was I going to let them in? I know, I'll run around to the back door, come through the house, and open the front door for them. I started running just as the police car pulled up, and one of the officers leaped out and raced after me, catching up just as I got inside. He slapped the handcuffs on me.

By this time, there were crimson stains all over the carpet. The cop leaned over and tried to revive Angelo, but it was too late.

At that point, Jean, who was seven months pregnant, came around to the front of the house, took in the scene with all of the police cars and everything, and fainted. I looked at her without feeling. Standing there in a daze, I realized the house was crawling with curious neighbors. Within fifteen minutes, the press and TV reporters had arrived. As I was led from the house, I noticed three police cars and six or more officers. Our nice, quiet neighborhood wasn't so quiet that morning.

They took me to the Burbank jail and booked me on a murder charge. The headlines said: BOOKIE PAL SLAIN, and GANGLAND SLAYING. Television and radio news reports were full of my story.

While I was in the Burbank jail, a minister visited me with a couple of other men. I didn't pay much attention to the line he gave me. He tried to tell me all about Jesus Christ. I didn't want to hear all that baloney, and to shut him up, I said, "You're too late, padre—I just killed a man."

"God will forgive you of that sin," he said, looking at me, his face registering no shock.

I answered with a sneer. "Man, you're crazy! God doesn't forgive anyone for killing anybody!"

The minister told me a story about the apostle Paul. Something about how he rounded up big crowds of Christians, and he'd have some of them killed, and he'd been forgiven. I got so disgusted, I turned my back and walked away.

But the story of Paul stuck in my mind. He'd killed some people, Christians even, and God had forgiven him—Maybe—maybe—

Everything else the preacher said was soon forgotten.

They transferred me to the Los Angeles County Jail after about four days. I was given a denim shirt and a pair of pants. All the new convicts were stripped and sprayed with DDT from head to toe, like a bunch of pigs. The stuff was really strong, and I was in agony for hours. I don't know about its potency for killing lice, but it sure killed my skin.

The jail was a hell—the mattresses filthy, the toilets even worse. There was no facility for doing any laundry, so some of the men washed their clothes in the toilet bowls. It was sickening. And the food was terrible, especially after the gourmet fare I'd grown used to.

When I was booked in, they stamped my ID envelope with a red star and placed it in my top pocket. I learned later that this was a label to remind them that I was to be watched a bit closer than the others, because I had been charged with first-degree murder and refused bail.

The conditions there disgusted me. I saw eighteen-year old boys—who had stolen parts from cars—thrown into the same tank with all the older, hardened criminals, crowded in with men charged with murder, rape, narcotics raps, and every crime you could name. Some of these had spent ten years in prison waiting for retrials on their murder cases. But the worst, to me, were the sex degenerates. To submit these raw, lost kids to that sort of filth was enough to turn my stomach. I'm sure

29

exposure to hardened criminals started most of the kids off on a new road to crime.

With many of the men, prison was a way of life. In this foul, crowded place, you could feel the hate. All they talked about was revenge and revolution. And how they despised the police! There was no rehabilitation there. It was a training camp for making these criminals harder and more down on society in general. No wonder these guys were ten times worse when they came out!

My chief attorney was Russell Parsons, the man who later was to defend Sirhan B. Sirhan, the man convicted of shooting Robert Kennedy. Mr. Parsons was an old hand at murder trials. My other attorney was Harry Weiss, who had represented many big movie stars. I had recommended him to many people in the past, and we had been acquainted for some time. Also, he had met Angelo on several occasions and didn't think much of him. Maybe that was why he offered to handle my case without a fee. I admired him a great deal. He knew how to get things done. With his staff of twenty-five people, he could take care of almost twenty-five cases a day.

I gave the attorneys the details about what had happened that day I shot Angelo. They went to see my wife and look over the evidence, then brought her back to the jail to see me. Poor Jean! She was so sad and distraught. All this nightmare happening when she was so soon to have another baby.

What a wonderful combination of attorneys! They complemented each other well. Parsons was quiet, deliberate, and serious. Weiss was a jovial, dynamic man who reminded me of a jackrabbit, always jumping around and getting things in motion. I liked to kid them. They couldn't understand how I could joke when I was facing the gas chamber. But it was just my sick mind making me put up a false front.

The days in jail seemed endless. Can you imagine being in a six-by-nine cell with four other men? There were bunks for only four of us, so one man slept on the floor. The stench was terrible. We were allowed showers once a week and at that time got a change of shirts and trousers. The underwear you were stuck with—and it got pretty gamy.

I'd listen to the guys talking about the charges that had put them in jail: possession of drugs, armed robbery, attempted murder, holdups, knifings. They all had one thing in common with the convicts I'd been locked up with before. They were all jailhouse lawyers with all kinds of tips on how to handle their cases. They thought they were so smart, but here they were behind bars.

As I lay in my bunk at night in those dismal surroundings, listening to the flushing of toilets echoing from every cell and hearing the screaming and yelling back and forth among the inmates, my mind wandered back through my life. I thought of my mother and father and how they had been struggling all those years. One reason I'd wanted to make a lot of money was to give them a few good years before they were too old to enjoy them. I remembered how my mother would often go to bed at night hungry so the meager food could be divided among the rest of the family. And dad struggling home with wood he'd gathered from the riverbank, then sawing it up for fuel so that we could keep warm. I thought of all the patched clothes I'd worn, handed down from one kid to another. And the holes in our shoes that dad was forever trying to cover so they'd last just a little longer.

I wasn't going to have my kids go through any of those hardships. I'd always find some racket to bring in plenty of money. And one day I'd send my folks enough to come out to California so I could show them a good time. All they had known was hard work. Dad had never been to a ballgame, had never been fishing. He and I had never had a real closeness. All we had done together was work—tending the garden or picking coal—and eat our meals at the same table.

31

Then my mind would snap back to that horrible day I shot Angelo. Joe Donato, the smart operator, was in jail on a murder charge! I didn't want to be a born loser like the rest of those guys, but here I was. I couldn't forget, either, that I was out on bail on a bookmaking charge that was still pending. That wasn't going to help me any. How had I gotten into such a mess?

I started looking for ways to avoid the death penalty. What if something went wrong in the trial? There was Angelo's wife. To me, she'd always be a mean, evil witch. I knew she'd give me trouble at this trial. And what about Angelo's friend, Louie? When he got out of jail, he'd be sure to stand up for his old pal. I could spend the rest of my days behind bars even if I didn't get the death penalty.

As I lay tossing on that broken-down mattress, I relived the day when I had shot Angelo. Remembering the sweat running down my forehead, the damp clothes clinging to my body, I broke out in a cold sweat again.

In the morning, I was to be taken to Burbank to appear in court.

4

Early on the day of my arraignment, twelve of us prisoners were handcuffed, put in chains, and marched
down to a bus. At the Burbank jail, we were put in the
holding tank to wait for our time in court. I listened to the
guys talk. It was the same old thing: what they were going to do when they were out of prison. They were all
going to hunt up their old buddies and get back in the
same old groove. A few of them talked about being with
their wives again.

Then the door was unlocked, and two detectives took
me out and led me through a long tunnel to the crowded
courtroom. As I glanced around, I recognized many familiar faces.

The court was called to order, and the judge read the
charge. "Joseph Daniel Donato, you are charged with
first-degree murder in that you killed a fellow creature
on this earth." That's not how he said it, but that's what
he meant. The words hit me like a sledgehammer. This

was no dream! I was there in the court, facing possible death.

Looking at me with tear-filled eyes was my wife, Jean, in the front row with my brother.I gave her a half-hearted smile.

Then all of a sudden, out of nowhere, Angelo's wife appeared. She charged down the aisle of the courtroom, screaming hysterically.

"Murderer! Murderer! You killed my husband! You murdered my husband!"

The bailiff and two detectives moved fast to drag her from the courtroom, but her screams could be heard even then. The place was in an uproar. The judge pounded his gavel to restore order. After all had quieted down, my attorney asked the judge if I could be released on bail since my wife was pregnant, not at all well, and expecting very soon. He also stressed that my victim had invaded the privacy of my home in a rage. His motion was denied.

As the detectives returned me to my cell, Angelo's wife's screams echoed in my mind. She was really crazy, I thought. Maybe she had made an impression on the judge. Suddenly my trial took on new complications.

I looked around the cold cell and felt real panic. There had to be a way out of all this mess! Then I remembered the act I had put on in the Army, faking insanity. I had achieved my purpose then. And it was a life and death matter I was facing now.

I got out of my bunk and threw myself on the floor in a state of hysteria.

"Don't shoot!" I yelled. "Don't come any closer, Angelo! Don't shoot!"

I lay there as if semiconscious, rolling my head back and forth. Then I heard the first gate open leading to my cell block.

It was the guard. "What's the matter, buddy? What you doin' on the floor?" He reached through the bars and shook me. The more he shook me, the more I screamed in hysteria.

"Don't come closer! Don't come any closer, Angelo!"

I figured it was working, because the guard said, "Don't worry, buddy. I'm going to get a doctor."

Within three minutes, there were seven or eight people clustered around me. As I lay on the floor, putting on my convincing act, someone held smelling salts to my nose. When I took my time reacting, they slapped the sides of my face smartly.

I heard one cop say, "This guy is crazy. He can't hear a word we're saying."

Before long, I heard the wail of the siren on the ambulance. I thought, Great! I'm going to make it to the nut department of the hospital. They really think I'm crazy.

As the ambulance drivers wheeled me out the front entrance on the stretcher, I could hear the sighs, the "ohs" and "ahs" of the bystanders. One man remarked, "The guy's crazy!" I smiled inwardly. All this would be on record now.

It was a long trip to the Los Angeles County Hospital, and the ambulance attendants kept telling me, "You'll be all right, pal. You'll be all right. You're going to the hospital."

In the emergency room, the doctors examined me. Everyone kept talking in a whisper. "This guy killed his bookie pal. But you can see he's crazy. He doesn't know where he is."

To myself, I rejoiced; it was working!

The doctor held smelling salts to my nose, and the fumes really opened up my head. I "woke up" and started screaming. Then I felt a hypodermic needle go into my arm.

I woke up five or six hours later in the County Hospital's jail ward. I'd made it! There were twenty-five other people in the large room. Although I was groggy, I felt quite comfortable. And it was all on the record that I was out of my head.

I was treated well during my hospitalization. In fact, the nurses were especially kind and thoughtful. To my left was a man who'd been shot in a liquor store holdup. He'd been lying there for months, crippled from a bullet in his spine. I felt sorry for him—a nice-looking black fellow of about twenty-eight or so. He'd probably be crippled the rest of his life. What would he have gotten out of the liquor store? $50? $100? In a way, it was too bad the bullet hadn't found his head. He'd be out of his misery.

The guy on my right whispered to me, "Say, buddy. Tell the nurse you can't sleep tonight. When she brings you the sleeping pills, slip 'em to me!" I guess this creepy guy was hooked on pills. I didn't need any. I was still dopey from whatever they'd had in the needle.

Before breakfast the second day, they brought in another patient—a guy who'd been shot about five times. He was white and still, and I figured he wouldn't make it through the day.

The food at the hospital was as good as any you'd get in a restaurant. I thought to myself that I wouldn't mind spending a week or so there, just to rest up. The service was fine, and the nurses so pleasant and willing to do things to make us comfortable. They even brought us crackers and milk between meals. What a change from jail!

On the third day, they needed my bed, so I was sent back to County Jail. I hadn't seen a psychiatrist or had any insanity tests, nor did I have any at a later time, but the hospitalization was on my trial record, and that was all that mattered. When my attorneys visited me to see how I felt, I played it cagey, for I sensed they had fallen for my act, too.

It was not easy to stand prison life. Although I wasn't lily white, I got sick of the dirty language. The men on the thirteenth floor shouted filthy suggestions to the women on the twelfth. They'd talk through the heat pipes that went from floor to floor. Then there were the junkies, all looking like zombies, and absolutely not to be trusted. None of the inmates looked very healthy. I lost fifteen pounds in three weeks, and some of the men who'd been jailed much longer were skin and bones.

One morning, my attorneys paid me a surprise visit and gave me the good news. Due to my wife's pregnancy, my mental condition, and Angelo's invasion of my home, I was going to be released on bail. I was the happiest guy in the world! I even heard myself saying, "Thanks, God!" as I went back to my cell. The words just seemed to slip out unconsciously.

News travels fast in prison. The inmates gathered around to congratulate me on getting out on bail. All of them wished they could walk out with me. I took a last look at them, realizing the poor losers would be spending years there or in other jails. I hoped I'd never see the inside of a cell again!

Two of my brothers were waiting for me as I stepped out into the warm sunshine. They remarked about how thin and pale I was. The ride home was beautiful. I took in every tree and shrub, every house and skyscraper, the sky, the clouds. I felt free and wonderful. It was like coming from hell to heaven. Even the smog smelled good!

Being home again was a great relief, but I started right in plaguing my wife. Although she was kind and understanding and showed great love and concern for me, I took this tenderness as weakness on her part. Her face reflected the stress and worry she was going through, but I was so completely focused on myself, I was blind to her real feelings.

While I'd been in jail, Tommy and Bloomie had looked after my interests. After all, business had to go on as usual. I found I had a more important reputation among the gang now. I was Joe Donato, the killer. Some of the boys threw some dinners for me. I felt I was really growing into a power.

One day, I had a phone call from Johnny Batina, a well-known underworld figure. He had been scared of Angelo, and was glad to see him dead. He offered money to me to fight my murder rap, but I refused it. In our world, when you turn down help, it shows you are strong.

On February 20, 1962, John Glenn became the first American to orbit the earth in a spacecraft. And on this day, Jean presented me with a son. We named him John Glenn. I was excited over the birth of my son, but the demands of business kept me from spending much time thinking about it.

One night, I met Bloomie and Tommy to talk over how things were going. We were together for several hours; then I got into my car and started home. As I drove away from the curb, I noticed another car which seemed to be following me. I drove onto the freeway, and sure enough, that car was still behind me. I speeded up. The other car kept up with me. I could see there were two men in it. Getting panicky, I drove down an off-ramp in the valley and headed for a convenient alley. Right behind me was the other car, speeding as fast as I was.

I began to think that maybe a contract had been put out on me, or maybe Angelo's wife or some of his friends were out to kill me.

I went in and out dark streets with the other car seven or eight feet from my rear bumper. If I could only see a cop! I looked everywhere for a police car. They'd help me, I knew. Suddenly I made a turn and found myself on a dead-end street. My heart pounded. If only I had a gun! I felt under the seat as I put on my brakes. Nothing. It was the end of the road.

Immediately, the two men stopped their car behind me and leaped out.

I looked around for a rock, a brick—anything. But there was nothing in sight. The men started to run toward me, their silhouettes looming in the headlights. This was it!

Then I heard the sweetest words I'd ever heard! "We are police officers. Stand still!"

They couldn't know how happy I was to see them! I was searched and questioned about my erratic driving. I explained why I'd been in such a panic—both of them were in plain clothes, and I had had no way of knowing they weren't paid killers from the underworld.

They had me park my car and took me to the Los Angeles Detective Bureau for more questioning. It was the same old routine: "Where were you? What are you doing?" Etc., etc., the same old rigmarole. But I didn't care; I was relieved to be alive! They released me, and I called Bloomie to pick me up and take me back to my car. I was still trembling when he got there.

I was to experience this same routine—"the roust"—from the police many times in the next five years.

Returning home, I explained to my wife what had happened. Jean was already a nervous wreck, and this episode didn't help any. She was a good wife and mother. Our house was kept clean and neat, and she took care of our little daughter and baby son with love and devotion. I knew she stuck by me because of the kids—but also because I was in trouble and she had great compassion.

That night in bed, I had one terrible dream after another. I dreamed I was in a war as a machine gunner. The enemy kept coming closer and closer. I turned my machine-gun on them and mowed them down! But more kept coming, and I was running out of ammunition. Then someone shot me. . . . In another scene, I saw two men walking toward my bed with their hands reaching for me. I woke up screaming and reached for a gun. I always slept with a gun on each side of the bed. My wife jumped up and turned on the light to see what was wrong.

I was to have these nightmares—and worse ones—for many years. Gone were those beautiful dreams of flying I'd had as a kid. Fear was building up inside me, becoming a twenty-four-hour part of my being. I hated to go to sleep—I knew I'd see those two men standing by my bed again, reaching down to grab me.

After many court appearances, my trial was postponed, but still I couldn't relax. I was constantly on my toes, watching for friends of Angelo—or anyone else who wanted me wiped out. Now and then, I went to one of our gambling establishments just to look in awhile. But I had to be careful the police weren't checking on me.

The phone rang one day after I'd been to one of our operations, and the caller identified himself as a vice cop. He said he wanted to talk to me. I tried to find out what it was all about. All he would say was that it was something very important, and he wanted to set up a meeting with me. I didn't trust any cop, but I met him that night, mainly out of curiosity.

The cop told me everything I'd done, everywhere I'd been that day. He said he'd been going to raid the gambling establishment with some other cops. The only reason they hadn't was because they'd had no use for Angelo and were almost grateful he'd been wiped out. If they'd raided the place while I was there, my bail would have been revoked. Then I'd have been out on three cases: bookmaking, murder, and gambling.

"So you saved my life," I told him. "Thanks a lot. How much do you want?"

"Nothing."

"Nothing?"

Then he told me I must be crazy. "You've got a nice wife and two nice kids. But you still haven't learned your lesson."

Maybe he wanted me to be a stool pigeon for the police department. Maybe that was why he wanted to see me.

He went on. "I have a favor to ask of you, Joe."

Here it comes. "What is it, cop? What do you want of me?"

He told me about a tragedy that had happened a few months before. A building had completely burned down, and in the ashes were found the remains of a man identified as Marty. I knew who he was referring to. Marty had bought a business, and it wasn't doing too well, so he took out a lot of insurance on the building with the idea of staging a fire to collect the money. But instead of getting a professional torch man, he had tried to do the job himself. Marty didn't know too much about the chemicals he was using. He had spread them all over the building. Evidently, before he got to the door, either the nails in his shoe created a spark or possibly the phone rang. Either would have been enough to ignite the chemicals. In a matter of seconds, the place was an inferno. The investigator for the insurance company had found Marty's car across the street, and there were chemicals in it. They refused to pay a dime on his policy.

But now it seemed that the police were puzzled over Marty's death. They had to know if it was accidental, or if he had been murdered and the fire set to cover it up. I was glad to be able to set the record straight with the information I had from underworld gossip.

The cop and I parted real friends. He was a rough, tough man, but a square shooter. He had the reputation of always getting his man, and a lot of the boys feared him. But he would never frame a guy.

5

It was nearly a whole year after I'd been released on bail that my trial finally came up. The first day was cloudy and drizzly as we approached the cold gray stone court building. Jean was at my side. "Keep her with you at all times," my attorneys had said. "Everyone will be looking at her and sympathizing with her."

In the elevator on the way up to the courtroom on the eighth floor, two women stood in front of us, and it was impossible to keep from hearing their conversation.

"Did you hear who's slated as prosecutor in the new murder trial in 840?"

"No, who?" The first woman named a well-known California prosecutor.

"You're kidding!" said her friend. "I wonder why they're bringing up their big gun? I thought it was just a guy shooting his friend in his living room."

For the first time since the shooting, a fleeting doubt crossed my mind. Did they have some evidence I didn't know about? Surprise witnesses? No, impossible. Angelo and I were the only ones in that living room. And Angelo was dead.

All courtrooms are dismal to me, places of execution. A defendant goes in there a free man, and when it's over, he goes out a prisoner for five, ten, sometimes thirty years or for the rest of his life. Sometimes he goes to the gas chamber.

My spirits picked up with the selection of the jury, and I took a real interest in trying to analyze each prospective juror being considered. The routine was the same for each one: Name? Occupation? Do you have any personal objection to capital punishment? and so on. This one was a bartender—good, he was a rounder. That one was once an air-raid warden—get him off; all air-raid wardens were frustrated policemen. (He got picked to be the foreman). It didn't seem they'd ever find enough satisfactory people, but by the third day, they had impaneled a full jury.

As I entered the courtroom the day we were going to get into the proceedings, I was actually glad to be getting the case under way. The looming trial had been like a chain around my neck.

The prosecutor was badly crippled with arthritis, but instead of feeling sorry for him, I thought, This guy is going to take his aches and pains out on me. All morning, he related the events of the day I'd killed Angelo—how he'd come to my house, nice and peaceful and calm, with a smile on his face. Angelo's wife must have painted that picture for him. She was a good liar. The prosecutor told about the velocity of the bullet, the color of the gun case—a whole lot of incidental details that seemed pretty irrelevant to me. I sensed that he really didn't have a good case against me, so he was beating around the bush.

Part of the image I wanted to maintain was my fearlessness. And so it was business as usual, all during the trial. Every noon I would meet with my lieutenants, collect the day's take, discuss any decisions, and generally run things. My underworld friends would say, "Joe, you gotta be crazy to do that right while your trial is goin' on. If they catch you, you're done!"

"But they're not going to catch me," I'd reply with a shrug. And they would marvel at my cool.

When court was recessed at noon the first day, I was given a message that The Camel, one of my men, wanted to talk to me. I met him down on Ninth Street on my two-hour break. He looked a mess! His lips were split open, and his nose all puffed up. It seemed that Holly, a muscleman, had been trying to shake Camel down for some money. Camel had refused, and so had received a good beating. Holly was an ex-fighter, and a lot of people feared him. The Camel was no match for him, since he weighed only a hundred and fifteen pounds. He had run to me for help, and I could see he was scared to death. Holly had a lot of enemies, and I could be counted in with them. But he also knew I was going through a murder trial and couldn't do anything to him at that time. Well, we would see about that. I told the Camel not to worry about a thing, and returned to the court for the afternoon session.

The first witness was a policeman from Burbank. He told how he'd received a call on that fatal morning, and when he got to my house, I had been running down the driveway. He described finding Angelo bleeding, in a state of shock; how he'd asked Angelo what had happened and got no answer. I admired the way he handled the questions.

The second cop on the stand told pretty much the same story. He said that he had handcuffed me, then later had found the murder weapon. After these testimonies, court was adjourned for the day.

All afternoon, I kept thinking of my friend The Camel and his battered face. After dinner, I made some phone calls and set an appointment to meet Holly. Later that night, we faced each other in a restaurant, and I heard his side of the story. He said The Camel had gotten smart with him. Knowing I didn't dare do anything to jeopardize my murder case, he was cocky and aggressive. The first thing I knew, he'd pulled a knife on me. But he must have smelled a rat, for he ran out of the place just before the cops came. Someone must have tipped them off. I told the cops I didn't know this character Holly. They tracked him down a block away, but he had gotten rid of the knife, so they let him go.

The trial went on and on. Finally, Angelo's wife was called to the stand. She told how her husband had left the house that last morning in a happy mood. She vowed there was no animosity whatsoever in the man, that he was just paying me a friendly visit.

"That man," she screamed, pointing at me, "that man murdered my husband!"

Again, there was an uproar in the courtroom.

My lawyers did their best to trip her up. But it was no use. She was a convincing liar. She'd made up a good story and was going to stick to it.

I began to really worry about the way things were going. It was possible I'd end up in the gas chamber. I had to think of another trick to get sympathy, so I started shedding copious tears. I realized I'd not get much compassion from the jury if I sat there looking like a wise guy.

One day, something rather unusual happened. After court was over, I was about to get into an elevator with my wife. Two jurors got in with us. They looked at Jean and me and smiled. One of them put her hand on my shoulder and told us to pray to God that everything would be all right. As we got out of the elevator and parted, they both smiled, and one even gave a knowing wink, assuring me they were on my side.

This little episode took a load off our minds. And this

had happened before the jurors had heard my side of the story. As we walked from the courthouse to get into our car, I started to laugh. "It was the tears," I told my wife. "They really got to the jury. I'll have to remember to bring two handkerchiefs tomorrow."

I always took credit for anything that went right, and when things went wrong, I could always find someone else to blame. That night, I relaxed with a couple of cocktails before dinner, and had several glasses of wine as I enjoyed my steak. This was becoming a trend. I was drinking more than ever.

Bloomie and Tommy, my two partners, came by the house to discuss our gambling and bookmaking business. They had plenty of know-how in our operations, but they lacked the guts to handle problems when the use of a lead pipe or baseball bat was called for. And, too, they themselves were gambling addicts. They made thousands of dollars, but were always broke. They simply weren't able to take care of the action as I had done. I was all business and didn't get fouled up with gambling myself.

The next day in court, Angelo's wife returned to the witness stand. She appeared to be quite calm as she repeated her testimony regarding her husband's death. I sat looking at her, boiling inside. After she'd stepped down from the stand, my lawyers started our defense. Our first witness was Tommy, my partner. He told how Angelo had cut his face with a knife. The jury was allowed to get a good look at his scarred face after his testimony. There was no doubt he'd been telling the truth.

Then Cecil, my ex-father-in-law, was called to the stand. No one in the courtroom knew him. He testified that Angelo had been a violent, dangerous, and turbulent man. One time in Cecil's home, Angelo had threatened him with a knife, vowing to cut out his spine. Thus far, no one had testified for the prosecution about how violent I was.

46

Another good witness for my cause was Meyer, an ex-fighter. He had seen Angelo cut up Tommy's face. The jury was sure to have compassion for Meyer, too, who struggled down the aisle on crutches.

Meanwhile, I was turning on the weeping act, until my lawyers told me I was overdoing it. When I was alone with them, I relaxed, making jokes.

Each day, as my lawyers brought more witnesses who attested to Angelo's mean character, I felt more secure. I would be so relieved when it was all over and I'd be perfectly free. There were many matters to be taken care of in my business.

One night, The Camel contacted me again. He wanted to let me know that the police had arrested Holly for beating him and trying to rob him. So—Holly was in jail. In the underworld, this is the wrong way to do things. You don't have your enemy arrested. You take care of him according to your own code. But The Camel was afraid; he wouldn't go home if he knew Holly was walking the streets. I had hoped he would calm down and lay low until my trial was over. Then Holly would get what was coming to him!

The next day, the trial resumed. I noticed a lot of the witnesses showed up day after day, interested in the final outcome of the case. I looked at the motley crowd and studied their faces, wondering why they weren't all out doing something more useful than sitting in that courtroom all day long.

Our first witness this day was Officer Colmbs, the cop who'd arrested me for bookmaking a few months before I killed Angelo. My attorney, Harry Weiss, had talked to him and learned the officer had been watching Angelo for months. He also testified that my victim had been a dangerous man. I admired Mr. Weiss for having found this valuable witness.

There was also a private detective who told about Angelo cutting Tommy's face—as well as a cop friend of

47

mine, Sergeant Haffer. He knew Angelo's background and reputation, and his testimony was very valuable, too.

The prosecutor did his best to break down my defense, to befuddle my witnesses, but they all held up well. I felt sure we'd win over the jury.

The night before Jean was to take the witness stand, she was terribly nervous and emotional. She couldn't eat a bite of dinner and was tossing and turning all night. As she took the stand the next morning, I was painfully aware of how shy and sensitive she was and what an ordeal this must be for her. She was serious and sincere as she told how she had been seven or eight months pregnant when the shooting had occurred. The whole scene came back to me as she described how she had heard the violent argument from the bedroom where she'd fled with our daughter. She said she couldn't hear all the conversation, but was terrified at its intensity. With tears streaming down her face, she told the jury how she had fainted away in the midst of it all, and the jury was visibly shaken.

Now it was up to my lawyers. I had dinner with them the night before I was slated to take the witness stand. The lawyers wanted me to be primed so my testimony would help us win the case. With them that night was a sharp young attorney named Dan Busby who had handled many cases for gamblers and movie stars. He went over the questions the prosecutors would be asking me the next day. He kept telling me it was up to me; I could win or lose my case—and my life. I liked this nice-appearing guy. He had a great sense of humor and a way with words. I was glad he was going to be in court the next day with Harry Weiss and Russell Parsons.

At home later, I felt calmer. I even thanked Jean for doing such a good job on the witness stand, and said I was sorry for treating her so badly, blaming it on my nerves. But in the back of my mind lingered the obsession that one of Angelo's friends was going to have my head blown off or my car rigged with a bomb. When you're playing with fire, you're always on guard, because you don't want to get burned. The timeworn quotations kept coming back to me: "Whatsoever you sow you will reap," and my father's, "If you live by the sword, you die by the sword." And I was still playing with fire. Every week I accepted the envelope of money from my partners in the gambling business, knowing I'd be in more trouble than ever if the police got wise to it.

As I took the stand in court the following day, a hush fell over the spectators. I hoped I'd play my role well. So much depended on my keeping my cool. After I was sworn in, I stated my name, wife's and children's names, and answered the rest of the routine questions. Then the prosecutor showed maps and layouts of my home. On a large chart tacked to a bulletin board in front of the jury was a sketch of our house with the footage of every room, the location of every piece of furniture, and every door and window. The prosecutor started off in an easy, polite manner. I knew he was trying to get me so relaxed I'd be off guard and possibly make a slip that would destroy my plea of self-defense.

My lawyers managed to keep the gambling and bookmaking part of our lives entirely out of the case. The judge ruled that the killing had been the result of a personal argument and had nothing to do with our illegal activities, which were therefore inadmissible as evidence. I knew that the prosecutor had argued privately time and time again with my lawyers, wanting to bring up my criminal background. My advisors knew that if Angelo's and my business connections were to be brought up in the case, it would look as if I had killed him in order to take over the whole operation. The district attorney's office was convinced the latter was true.

During the day, a lot of confusing questions were thrown at me. The judge warned the prosecutor to get to the point. The State's case involved going over and over the type of rifle I had used, the velocity of the bullet, and other details related to my weapon. Often, my attorneys objected. They reminded the prosecutor that I had admitted killing Angelo; that the State didn't have a strong case against me, and so was trying to distract the jury with irrelevant facts.

I found myself studying each juror. One man wasn't impressed with my tears. He was a miserable-looking person. I'd have wagered he'd hang his own mother. All through the trial, I felt a great animosity toward this creep.

The courtroom was a sort of theater, I felt, and I was on the stage playing a part. I even dressed for my role. Every day, I showed up in the same cheap suit. I wanted the jury to look at this poor, unfortunate slob and feel he'd been unjustly accused.

Angelo's wife didn't miss a minute of the trial. While I was testifying, I could see her rejoicing in my being dragged over the coals. How I wished she were in the box with Angelo, six feet under!

The prosecutor went over and over every word of my testimony. He kept telling the jury, "There's more to this case than meets the eye!" And repeatedly, my attorneys would raise objections to this innuendo, and the judge would remind the prosecutor to stick to the facts and not air his own opinions.

At the end of the day, my clothes were wringing wet. I had a prosecutor wanting to send me to the gas chamber, and twelve jurors watching every move I made and straining to hear every word I uttered. In front of me was my audience—friends, enemies, and strangers—all watching me constantly. And the ever-present, hate-filled eyes of Angelo's wife! Every day she stalked into the courtroom—a woman in black. I thought, "All she needs is a broom and a safety belt."

Throughout my testimony, I kept repeating, "He

threatened me. I was frightened . . . I was protecting my home—my loved ones!" I told the jury that I had seen Angelo cut a man's face with a knife; that I knew he had been involved in killings back East. I tried to paint myself as a square kind of guy—home-loving and church-going—who wouldn't kill a flea. What a joke!

Finally I heard the statement I thought would never come: "No more questions," and I left the stand. Both sides would sum up their cases on the following day. The trial was about over. As I drove home with Jean, I felt the pressure was really off, and I could see the look of relief in her eyes, too. All we had to worry about was the jury. How would the final arguments affect them?

After dinner that night, there were many phone calls from friends telling me how glad they were that the trial was about over. Many gave their opinions on the various testimonies, and all were sure it looked favorable for me. The underworld was watching my trial closely, and I was very pleased with myself.

The Big Day was warm and pleasant, and I took it as a favorable omen. When Jean and I went up in the elevator, three of the jurors were also passengers. This time they were grave and unsmiling. This was a big day for them, too.

All during the prosecutor's summation, he repeated his old line, "There's more to this case than meets the eye!" He stressed the fact that Angelo had not been armed; that he had come to my home peacefully for a friendly visit. He talked about the velocity of the bullet and the caliber of the rifle. He even referred to my weeping, warning the jury that it was an act to win them over. His strong argument was that this had been an ambush-type killing, prearranged. For that reason, he argued, it was first-degree murder.

Then my attorneys had a chance to refute these charges. They showed how vicious Angelo had been and reminded the jurors that a man of Angelo's violent nature can become deadly at any moment. They dwelt on the fact that I was defending my home, my family, and my life, that anyone under the same strain and tension might pull the trigger without realizing what he was doing.

The arguments continued all day. The judge was to give the jury its final instructions the following morning. That night, I took the usual sleeping pills, wanting to blank the trial from my mind. I dreamed I was with Adolf Hitler, traveling through Europe in an open car, conquering everything in sight. What a dream to have the night before I'd learn my fate!

The following morning, we listened to the judge instruct the jury to bring a first-degree murder verdict which would mean the gas chamber for me. Or they could bring in a verdict of acquittal. After two hours of detailed instructions, the jury was led out to start their deliberations.

Five hours went by, and there was still no word from the jury room. Deep down inside, I had never had any real doubt that they would be unable to agree on a conviction for first-degree murder without a whole lot more evidence than they had. And that was the reason why I could remain so outwardly cocky throughout, so cool in playing my role, so calm in directing the affairs of my business.

But now I started to wonder. It was impossible, of course, that the verdict could be anything but acquittal. But why was it taking so long? What if— I forced the thought out of my mind.

On the second day of waiting, I strolled to within earshot of the jury room and heard loud yelling between a man and a woman. Try as I might, I couldn't make out what they were saying. I thought of those two women on the elevator so long ago, and wondered if the creep I despised was browbeating one of them. I hoped they were still in sympathy with me and were not going to allow themselves to be easily swayed.

After three and a half days, the judge called the jurors into the courtroom. They were hopelessly deadlocked—ten for acquittal and two for conviction.

After it was all over, many of the jurors gathered around us. They talked to my wife and my attorneys and were especially kind and frank in their remarks to me. Some of the spectators lingered nearby, wanting to be in on the excitement of my victory. I noticed Angelo's wife as she left the courtroom, her face contorted with rage.

As Jean and I drove home that night, I hoped with all my heart that I wouldn't be back in the courtroom again. The State could ask for a retrial, but for now, I was free on bail. I felt as if I'd been loosened from heavy shackles! I promised Jean that life would be better for us now, and I meant it sincerely.

6

Back in Pennsylvania, my mother had learned of my trial indirectly and had finally told my dad. Naturally, it was a shock to them. Some of their other sons had been in trouble through the years. Carl was a drifter, and although not a violent man, he'd had a few brushes with the law. Pasquale had been a bit of a worry, too, but had settled down in a good job selling advertising. The family called him "The Intellectual."

Unlike me, my bartender brother, Ralph, avoided bursts of rage, but became quite a wheeler-dealer. Tony had been a hardworking foreman in a factory for many years and he had a fine family. Nor did my family have to worry about Frankie, who had a good office job with the telephone company.

My younger brother, Charles, had tried to follow in my footsteps, but this was cut short after some convictions for gambling. Then he became seriously ill, and the family was really worried about him. I urged him to move his family to Los Angeles. I wanted to be able to watch him and keep him straight.

After the strain of my trial had ended, it seemed a good time to keep my promise to my parents. I'd always told them I'd bring them to visit California, so they could bask in the sun and enjoy themselves for a change. And so I did. What a joy it was to take them to Disneyland and watch their faces light up like children's! They loved the ocean and the tropical scenery so unlike Pennsylvania. The climate and the change of pace agreed with them, and my brother and I urged them to move to Los Angeles, but after their visit, they headed home.

My mother and father were worried about the life I was living. Mother said she'd been praying for me to get out of my criminal activities. Dad was particularly emphatic in his arguments.

"Son, some day soon, if you don't quit what you're doing, one of your friends will put a bullet in you. I can look through you. You're wild and unhappy. Quit, son! Get out of this racketeer life. You have some money saved. Be smart, or you'll wind up dead or in jail for life."

Until the day he died a year later, dad preached to me to quit my illegal rackets and turn legitimate. I felt his passing deeply, remembering him working day and night to keep his family together, recalling all the hardships he'd lived through. But I couldn't help also recalling the times when I was a kid when dad seemed to reject me. When I was fourteen, I heard dad say, "I don't like him. I don't like him!" when someone called him down for ignoring me. I tried very hard to earn his love and felt that someday I'd be able to prove I'd make good. Then I could make things easier for him and my mother. Now it was too late. If only they had stayed in California, he might have lived much longer.

I was soon active again in my business. It was good to be back in action. I had more prestige in the underworld now that I was a killer. Although my bookmaking trial was still pending, and I had to be cautious, crime was my way of life. Bloomie, Tommy, and I bought a club at Third and Lucas in Los Angeles. We had card tables and on the side conducted bookmaking and gambling. Soon our business was booming. We posted NO GAMBLING signs all over the place, which was a joke. Now and then we were visited by honest policemen trying to make arrests. Whenever they showed up, they'd have trouble getting in because we were a private club. In the meantime, everyone would be warned, and the gambling sheets and other telltale items would be hidden.

Some of the gamblers at the club would play cards for as low as a dollar a game and some for as high as five thousand. Many horse players bet up to a thousand dollars on one horse. On fight nights, gamblers arrived from all over to watch boxing on television. We would charge each person a fee to watch the fight. Their bets ranged from two to five thousand dollars on a match. Many times there were tens of thousands of dollars wagered on big championship fights in our club. Usually the men stayed on to gamble, and some of these games involved as much as fifty thousand dollars.

Addiction to gambling can happen to anyone. It's a sickness, like alcoholism and drug addiction. Many have lost everything: families, business, homes, and their self-respect. Our clientele included all types—from pimps to doctors and lawyers.

Although I was busy again, I hadn't forgotten Holly. I was burned up over the way he shook people down and beat them up. No one had done anything about it, so I arranged another meeting with him at a restaurant. Our meeting, however, wasn't successful. He did a lot of yelling, and I couldn't reason with him.

I wasn't the only one who hated Holly's guts. The Camel's pal, Bob, had been boiling over the bad beating The Camel had taken. Bob was well over six feet tall and a muscular two hundred pounds. I was surprised he hadn't hunted up Holly to retaliate before now. I knew he hung around Harry's Bar, and I phoned the place a couple of months later.

The pay phone rang about eight times before Rickie, the bookie, answered. He recognized my voice. "What's up, chief?"

"Is Bob around?"

"Sure," he answered. "He's sitting here shooting the breeze."

"Jump in your car, Rick, and bring Bob along."

"Anything wrong?"

"H-O-L-L-Y," was my reply.

It wasn't long before we were together in my car. Bob chewed on his toothpick nervously and told me to cut down my speed.

"Lay it out, chief," he snapped.

We drove in a roundabout way for several blocks checking for police tails. I told them we were headed for the Merry-Go-Round Bar where Holly had been fingered.

"Gee, that joint is packed this time of day," Rick remarked.

"Don't worry," I assured him. "Everybody hates Holly's guts. Nobody will interfere."

The bar was crowded. Bob and Ricky casually entered wearing baseball caps and carrying bats. Holly got up to leave, and as he turned, he saw Rick and Bob not two feet away. He knew them well—who they were and with whom they were connected. In a second, Bob brought his bat down on Holly's head. The sound of a loud groan echoed through the bar. Holly slumped to the floor, blood rushing from his head. The place became very quiet. The bat came down again on Holly's form.

Bob and Rick looked everybody over calmly, then turned and very slowly walked out. Before the door had slammed shut behind them, Hank, the owner, was yelling, "Call an ambulance! He's bleeding! He's bleeding

57

all over my rug! My brand-new rug!"

The timing had been perfect. I picked up Bob and Ricky a short way from the bar.

"How did it go?" I asked.

"Boy! He hit a home run over Holly's head," Ricky replied with a forced smile.

"He may not pull through, chief," Bob murmured.

"Nobody will miss the bum!" I felt we'd achieved a lot. We drove around awhile, then I crammed a few hundred-dollar bills into Bob's hand. "Get lost for a week," I ordered.

Bob took off his baseball cap, combed his hair neatly, and said, "Drop me off here. See you guys in a week."

Rick was nervous and sweating profusely. Bob looked cool and calm. As I let Rick off, I slipped him some money and told him to lay low for a few days.

As he walked away, I said, "Oh, well . . . Another day's work!"

Two hours later, some policemen knocked at the door of my home. They told me that Holly had been badly beaten and was dying. I was also advised that I was the prime suspect.

"Now, listen," I told them. "Holly was a nice guy, and I'm sorry he got beat up. But I don't know anything about it."

They were sure I was lying.

I went on. "If you have any witnesses, get on with your case. Otherwise, I'll ask you to please leave."

As they turned to go, I added, "Poor Holly! What a terrible thing to happen!"

The next few days, the bookies were laying odds that Holly wouldn't last through the week. But he did survive, after spending several weeks in the hospital being treated for a broken wrist, broken arm, and a severely fractured skull.

Some time later, Holly appeared on a well-known TV newscast and stated that he'd been beaten up by two of

Joe Donato's boys. During the ten minutes they allowed him on the air, he described how brutal I was. I understand the station had a call after the broadcast warning them not to use my name without proof. The repeat of Holly's interview was run with my name beeped out.

The following week, I met my friend Sergeant Haffer at a Chinese restaurant. Here was a real man—well-educated and in good physical condition. Given a few more years in the police department, he could have become one of the top men. He had connections with a few key people in City Hall, and these were hard to find, as City Hall was getting cleaned up by the Police Intelligence Squad and Internal Affairs Bureau. Haffer and I had been meeting for quite some time, and I always had a little gift for him. He was a good man for favors, if the price was right.

As we sat down, he said, "Joe, that Holly is in bad shape. But, of course, he had it coming."

I didn't say a word.

He went on. "The story is that some of your boys did the job."

"Sarge, you know me better than that! I hate violence."

We both burst into laughter.

Haffer had the phone numbers of our gambling and bookie offices, and it was his job to tip us off if we were going to be raided. He carried the numbers in a little black book in his jacket pocket.

"Say, Haffer," I said. "Suppose somebody gets ahold of that book?"

"Don't worry, Joe. I've got it in code."

As we were leaving the restaurant, a black and white police car drove up. It was Officer Rossi, in civilian clothes and drunk as a skunk. He was in on the take and had some conversation with Haffer, then staggered away.

As I got into my car, I turned to Haffer and said, "That

guy is gonna cause an explosion. You can't trust a drunk."

"He's gonna be all right, Joe. You worry too much. I'll have a talk with Rossi."

Things went smoothly for a few months. Business was booming; everybody was making lots of money, and my connections were getting bigger than ever. One afternoon I was at the YMCA playing handball, which was my second love—money being the first. I took my shower and steam bath and was about to leave when the P.A. system blurted out, "Joe Donato wanted on the phone. Emergency call."

I ran for the phone.

It was Dick, one of my associates. "Joe, get over here quick! Our joint and the bookie offices have been raided! Man, it's been well-planned and executed!" He was frantic.

I met Dick in ten minutes. He was pale and shaking. He told me how he had just missed getting pinched in a bookie office by a carload of vice cops. I couldn't believe it! I immediately tried to get Sergeant Haffer on the phone, being careful to disguise my voice. I knew he'd have the answer. I called all over, but he was nowhere to be found.

All of my associates were puzzled. Not one joint had been tipped off by Haffer. He'd never crossed us up before. I thought of the double cross for a moment. It couldn't have been Haffer! He was too smart for that.

For two days, we couldn't locate either Haffer or Rossi. Then the headlines told the story: VICE DEPARTMENT SHAKE-UP. TWO OFFICERS ARRESTED FOR TAKING BRIBES. Rossi had gotten drunk and popped off to some young detectives about how much money he was making on the side, and he had involved Haffer in his drunken outburst. The young ambitious detectives didn't lose any time in reporting the conversation to the Police Internal Affairs Bureau.

60

For the next two weeks, Rossi's phone was tapped while the two young detectives picked his brains. They set a trap for Sergeant Haffer, without the knowledge of anyone in the Vice Department. Then they sprang it.

Haffer and Rossi were arrested and held incommunicado for two days. They took Haffer's little black book with all our numbers in it and decoded the whole thing. Haffer denied everything, but he couldn't explain away the phone numbers of the bookie offices. He told them he was going to bust these places in a few weeks and was getting ready to move in on them.

"Where did you get all the numbers of these bookie offices?" was the big question he was asked.

Haffer thought for a moment. "From an informer."

"Who?" the police asked.

"Joe Donato."

The police all laughed at him. "We know some of the joints *belong* to Joe Donato!"

But Haffer stuck to his story. It was the only one he had. Later, he was released on bail. The press spread his name all over the front page, and he was too hot to contact for a few days. But in a week, we arranged a meeting.

"Joe, you were right," Haffer admitted dejectedly. "That drunk Rossi ruined everything. I had to tell them you gave me the numbers, because I knew you'd back me up. Nobody else would." He was really feeling low, and I felt sorry for him.

He added, "The prosecution may subpoena you to court, Joe. You've got to back up my story!"

"What are you going to do about Rossi?" I asked. "He'll sing like a canary."

Haffer asked what I suggested doing.

"A one-way ride is the only answer, friend," I snapped back. "Think it over."

I talked to the boys about our conversation, and we agreed I should back up his story. After all, Haffer had been a star witness in my murder trial. Now he was getting all the headlines and coverage on radio and television.

But I managed several other meetings with him. Haffer was a strong, solid guy but very worried. He told me he didn't want Rossi taken for a ride. I remembered I'd never given Rossi any money, so I had nothing to fear from him.

Their trial lasted five weeks. Rossi talked, and they believed him, but they didn't fall for Haffer's story.

I felt sad when Haffer was found guilty and sent to prison. What a shame! He was a stand-up guy. But he had done business with a drunk. Even I knew that's bound to be dynamite!

I was having a real ball on the side, going deep-sea fishing at Catalina and off the coast of Mexico, rubbing elbows with some of the top people, including a few movie stars. At some of the beach spots, I did some fancy swinging with my private stock of women. My business was bringing in a generous income, and I was living like a king.

Then one day, I had a call from my attorney advising me that we were scheduled to go to court on the book-making charge. It had been pending since before I'd killed Angelo. The trial didn't take long. I was found guilty, given three years on probation, a fine, and a sus-pended sentence. The charge had been reduced to a misdemeanor.

I was glad to have this trial behind me, though it meant I'd have to be very careful for the next three years. It would mean staying very much in the back-ground unless some real heavy trouble came to our group.

Shortly after the bookmaking case was closed, I got together with Willie Alvarado, a bookie and gambler with whom I was to do business for many years to come. One day, Willie came to me and told me about two meatballs (Italians, in his language) who had muscled in on his bookie business. He was so scared that he gave in to their demands.

About two months later, the same two men, Lennie and Tony, came into our club and beat up one of our members. This called for some action. They were considered tough guys, but Joe Donato could be tough, too! Tommy, Bloomie, another man, and I arranged a meeting with these two characters. They brought along a third party. The conversation was long and to the point. They wanted a piece of our gambling business. And we wanted no part of them.

I tried to be calm, but my temper flared up. They didn't know we'd brought a couple of guns with us. There was a violent argument, and Bloomie and I brought out our weapons. I put my gun right to the head of one of the men. If I hadn't remembered I was out on probation, I would have pulled the trigger on all three men. My plan called for them to be set up later at a "family meeting" where we'd do them in.

They left pronto—afraid for their lives. I wasn't to see them again for several months, and when I did, they acted like perfect gentlemen. It had been a slick try to move into our business, but it didn't work.

Sometimes I would make as much as five thousand dollars a week from my illegal activities, though usually it was considerably less. Once a month, I would report to my probation officer, and I realized from the start that I'd have to have a legitimate occupation to show I was going straight.

I arranged with the owner of a third-rate television store in downtown Los Angeles to put me on his payroll, and I'd show up at random times to work in the place. I received my regular paycheck with the usual deductions and began building up my Social Security—and a favorable reputation with the Probation Department. This also gave me a legitimate income for filing my tax returns.

I was to become well acquainted with some of the clients in my bookie business whom I would personally handle. One of my favorites was Leo, a "fish" by trade, a man who handled prostitutes. He had four or five girls working in different apartments and took fifty percent of their earnings. His connections with bellhops in big hotels provided many a lonely businessman with a luscious date.

Leo drove a big car, smoked the best cigars, and was addicted to betting on the horses.

I'd greet him with, "Hiya, sucker! You owe me five hundred bucks for last week's loss on the nags."

"Joey, one of these days, I'm gonna make a bit on you bookies. And you're gonna bring me a bagful of greenbacks!"

"When Abe Lincoln wakes up—that's when you'll win on the horses!" I'd retort.

Whenever Leo ran short of cash, I'd take it out in trade with some of his girls. And he was always losing money on the nags.

Another faithful client with a passion for betting on the horses was Abe, who was a successful women's clothing manufacturer in downtown L.A. He made some big hits through me over the years, but we bookies always wound up with the money in the end.

I often sent beautiful girls to Abe's place for him to outfit in clothes. He had an eagle eye for the gals and loved to party. The girls always knew Abe would be generous with them. He was a real lovable Jew. He died at the age of forty-one, his body full of cancer. I knew we all had to go sometime, but his death was a shock to me, as Abe seemed just in the prime of life.

My social business life was curtailed abruptly when my attorneys advised me that I was going to have to stand trial again for Angelo's murder. The proceedings went on much the same as they had at the first trial. This time, there was a new judge, Evelle Younger, who was

64

later to become Attorney General for the State of California.

My wife was by my side all through the hearing, and it was sheer hell for her. My whole way of life was repugnant to her, but she stuck by me for the children's sakes. She herself had been without a father since she was six, and she realized that having two parents was important, even though I was a poor excuse for a father and husband. I didn't want to be bothered with the kids, and they received no love or understanding from me. The family was well supplied with the necessities of life, but I didn't give them much of my time. When I was around the house, I treated them badly, using foul language, and even slapping my wife around.

The strain of the trial showed clearly on Jean's face. Day after day, she sat with the spectators, embarrassed and worried as she listened again to the gruesome details of the murder.

After the jury had received their instructions, we were both on edge wondering whether or not I would be found guilty. On the third day of the jury's deliberation, a very odd thing occurred. The panel was in the hotel on the way to their rooms when the elevator became stuck between the first and second floors. The guard accompanying them was carrying a pistol and, after all the panic buttons had been pushed to no avail, he had used his gun to open the trap in the ceiling. He then struggled through the opening and made his way to the upper floor. His pistol had been carelessly laid above the passengers, precariously aimed at them. They were all released unharmed, but the newspapers and radio gave it wide publicity.

After this episode, it was rumored that the jurors had learned something from the ordeal. If a sheriff could be that careless with his gun in an emergency, why couldn't Joe Donato have reacted as foolishly? Luckily, the police force doesn't have many such reckless cops.

On the third day of deliberation, I was acquitted. The jury all came over to embrace me after the case had ended, and some of the older women even kissed me. The spectators crowded around to shake my hand, and I left the courthouse cocky and pleased, giving myself all the credit for winning—as usual.

That night, the boys gave me a nice party. The wine was plentiful, the food was exquisite, and the celebration colossal. Nor did the festivities taper off soon. The following months were spent in a series of wild parties, getting loaded with alcohol and marijuana and associating with the wildest women I could find. It wasn't hard for me to attract women. When my hair started to gray, I kept it darkened, so I would still appear young and handsome. I was not tall—just five-feet-eight, and my weight at that time was a hundred and sixty-three pounds, but the women found me attractive. I was always the life of the party—joking, doing impersonations, telling jokes. I always laughed a lot. In fact, I'd get to laughing and couldn't stop. It must have been a sort of hysteria. The guys liked to have me at all the parties to keep things hilarious.

One of our favorite gathering places was "Sneaky Pete's" on the Sunset Strip. It wasn't a large, impressive place, but it had an underworld atmosphere that made us feel at home. The food was always delicious, and the service was great. Big Al, the owner, was a genial host and a real friend. "Sneaky Pete's" had been a haven for the swinging crowd for many years. Often movie stars dropped in to enjoy its unique atmosphere.

Through all of this fast-paced, high living, through all the laughs and good times, there were many times I felt an empty space inside. I was making more money than ever, but was not really happy. I was beginning to have terrible dreams and nightmares again: men coming at me with guns; my car being blown up with me at the wheel; someone stabbing me; being shot at through a

66

window. It seemed I was never to get any rest.

When I was finally off probation, I welcomed the chance to work off steam whenever my violent nature was aroused. One of my outbursts happened when Bloomie had an argument with a guy named Murray. I had a roll of dimes in my fist, and after a few hot words, I punched him in the face. Bloomie grabbed the guy and threw him to the floor. Breaking a glass, he pushed the jagged edges into Murray's face. The blood spurted upward as he lay writhing on the floor. Bloomie and I made a fast exit, and the incident was soon forgotten. I had released some of my hate and felt better.

One Saturday night, some of the fellows gathered at Eddie's Bar for a meeting and drinks. The place was crowded. The piano player kept banging out one loud number after another, and some of the customers were dancing. Eddie had been working for me, calling in bets on horses. During our discussion, one of our group, Johnny, went to the men's room. When he returned, he said, "Joe, there are three wise guys in there looking for trouble."

Eddie said, "Yeah, Joe. These are the three guys who want to rip up my bar. They're always looking for trouble."

As the meeting continued, the three men left my mind. Then a bartender came over to tell Eddie that they were giving everyone in the bar a rough time. I asked Eddie if he had a club or bat.

He, Johnny, Jumbo, and I left our table, and Eddie slipped me a bat he kept behind the bar. Armed with the weapon, I walked to the end of the bar where the three men were drinking.

"You're looking for trouble, fellows?" I asked. "Well, you've just found it!"

While the merriment went on in the place, Johnny took the baseball bat and came down with it on the head of one of the men. The other two lurched at us, but

Johnny managed to come down again on another skull. The two lay on the floor bleeding as the third man ran out the door. No one else left the bar. The piano player kept banging away, and the crowd kept dancing and singing in drunken hilarity.

We finished our drinks, washed our hands, and left. The wounded men were taken to the hospital some time later. I was never questioned, for no one would testify.

Another time, I worked over a certain Rocco with a lead pipe in a piece of rubber hose, after he'd made some remarks doubting my loyalty to crime and the underworld. I got real pleasure out of beating up that guy.

I had no fear of men larger than I was; it was the small ones I had to watch. Many of the most ruthless ones were small and used guns instead of fists.

About this time, we got into one of our most lucrative cons, one that employed my unique talent for impersonation. We would tell the rival bookie we wanted to set up that we were beginning to get some action from the studios, casually dropping the names of a few famous stars. And since he was a friend, if there was ever more than we could handle, we would send some of it his way. But whichever star it was, he would handle the actual transaction through a go-between at the studio (one of our boys), because the star didn't want to be seen associating with bookies.

A few days later, while our conversation was still fresh in the bookie's mind, I would call him up and impersonate a famous star rumored (by us) to put down a sizable bet or two from time to time. The bookie, who often himself had originally come West with some romantic notion of Hollywood, in his own eyes had finally arrived. He had so-and-so on the other end of this very phone.

Meanwhile, at my end, Tommy or Vince would be sitting next to me on a direct line to another accomplice at Hialeah or Aqueduct or Gulfstream, wherever we were going to have our star place his bet.

The moment we knew the winner of the race we were going to bet, Vince jotted it down on a pad in front of me, and I casually had our star get around to placing his bet.

We needed only thirty seconds to pull this off, and invariably the bookie would be so enthralled with talking to the star that he wouldn't be keeping that close track of the time. Somehow, they never seemed to catch on, though after a few months, word began to circulate through the underworld, "Don't take any bets from so-and-so or so-and-so! Those guys are past-posters! Why, they're nothing but crooks!"

Another trick we used to pull when we wanted to scare rival bookies: we'd have some of our boys pose as police detectives, complete with phony identification cards and badges. They would call on the gambler and give him a bad time.

"You're going to go to jail for bookmaking. Shall I put the handcuffs on him, sergeant?"

The guy would be so scared, he'd leave that location. And another rival would be canceled.

The more money I made, the more unhappy I was. And that just didn't make any sense. I had thousands and thousands of dollars, I didn't even know how much, stashed away. I could buy anything I wanted. I had beautiful women; all I had to do was say, "Hey. Come here." I had reputation, exactly the one I'd always wanted: that of a big man in the underworld. I had success—dozens of guys worked for me, and the operation was so smooth, it almost ran itself. And now plans were afoot with a man at the top of the family hierarchy for us to start bringing the independent bookies into our flock.

And I had power, *real* power. The power of life and death. I could end a human life just like that, with a snap of my fingers. Scores of guys feared me. (Of course, that kind of fear was bought at a price. I knew my own turn was long overdue. I'd get home at night, and before I

69

could get out of the car, another car might come down the street, and I'd duck down on the seat and die half a dozen times before it passed. And in the morning, when I put the key in the ignition, I'd wince and shrink away before I turned it.)

I had been happier when I was a kid back in Reading, walking around with cardboard in my shoes and sleeping three to a bed. We were together then, a real family, sharing—

Stop it, Joe! The hard side of me cut in. Thinking like that is weakness. You're being *weak*, Joe!

If there was one thing I detested in anyone, and especially myself, it was weakness. A man, a real man, was hard—like the cold steel of a gun barrel. You got soft, and you got dead; it was that simple. A matter of survival. So I hardened my heart wherever I detected softness.

And yet I wished I had never been born. Because this life was hell. Heaven came when life finally came to an end—then there was the peace of not having to live any longer. How I longed for it! I wanted my sentence on earth to be over. I wanted to go to bed and just not wake up in the morning.

And as if in answer to prayer one night, instead of light, fitful sleep, I fell into deep slumber and had a dream. I seemed to be in an operating room, looking down at myself stretched out on the table. I had been shot in the head, and I could hear the doctors saying there was no hope, nothing they could do.

All of a sudden, a beautiful ray of light, white with flashes of gold, came down on a forty-five degree angle to the operating table. I saw myself slowly rise out of that body, and then I joined completely with myself and began to lope up that shaft of light in a sort of slow motion. I felt so free. I thought, I'm going up. There's something up there! And I knew it was God.

After about five or six steps, the light became bright

and brilliant, the clouds white and fluffy, the sky azure blue, and the ray of light continued right on up. I felt brand-new inside— Why, death was wonderful!

I looked over my shoulder to the operating table, which I could still see in the distance, and there I was— at least my body was still lying there. I looked up again, and began loping higher, and God became more and more real.

When I looked back again, the body had already gone from the operating table to a coffin. People were gathered around, crying and weeping, and I thought, Oh, those poor people! I yelled back, "Don't cry! I feel wonderful! This is wonderful here!"

But a voice from beyond and within me said quietly, "Joe, they can't hear you."

I turned upward again, and I couldn't wait to get to the top. The higher I went, the wider the shaft of light became, till it seemed like I was in the middle of a broad highway. I ran faster, my hands in the air, so happy . . .

Then I woke up. To another day. Of the same old life.

7

My violent temper continued to get me into trouble. No one escaped my outbursts. The worst one happened three years after I'd killed Angelo.

My brother Pasquale, The Intellectual, was always bugging me about my way of life. One day he came to my home, and we got into an argument. As it became more bitter, he hit me in the mouth and ran out toward his truck. I tasted blood—how I hated it! I picked up the pistol I'd been using for target practice, followed my brother outside, and fired the two remaining bullets—carefully missing his head by twelve inches. I only wanted to scare him, and I was successful, for he jumped into his truck and raced away.

When the police arrived shortly, they said I'd tried to kill my brother. There was a bullet hole in his truck. I was arrested and booked for attempted murder. I was in jail for one day, but released when Pasquale decided not to prosecute. For years after, I wouldn't speak to him.

Business went on as usual. I'd be in one mess after another, but kept close to my associates and the action. Early in January, 1970, I got word that Angelo's old partner, Louie, had been released after serving many years in prison and was coming to California. Knowing about him, I was sure he'd want a piece of the action along the line somewhere. My first thought was that perhaps Louie was bent on revenge. I had to be very cautious from here on in. Louie was the best when it came to having guts and being ruthless in the underworld. He loved money, and if he could be handled, he'd be a tremendous asset on the West Coast.

If, however, he still had a lot of his old ways, he could be dangerous to have around. I pondered the question and finally called a meeting of some of the boys. A decision had to be reached, for I wanted to be the hunter rather than the prey as far as Louie was concerned.

I decided to contact Mr. Cigaro, who was one of the bigwigs on the coast. "Cigaro" was an appropriate name, as he was always chewing on a big stogie. He hated the Jews. I've heard him say, "The Italians plant the potatoes, and the Jews dig 'em up!" He was also feared by his associates. Although he was always laughing, he could kill without batting an eye. Cigaro had the final word in big decisions, and everybody abided by those decisions—or else.

Shortly after Louie came to town, Cigaro called a meeting with him and me and three other guys. We were a tense group—mostly murderers—who feared each other. But no one would have suspected it with all the back-slapping and laughter.

Cigaro had a habit of jumping in with answers to his own questions. "Angelo's dead, right? Right!" he began. "We're all together, right? Right!"

The others sat there like dummies, not having a chance to let out a peep. Cigaro went on with his plans for us.

"You agree, Joe? Right!" And so on. I felt I was going

to have a showdown with him someday.

Louie had an insatiable craving for action. He had plenty of money, but he kept talking about big bank jobs he was going to pull off. Cigaro told him he'd have to get that kind of business off his mind.

Louie was good-looking in a rugged way. And to think that at one time he'd had his head shaved for the electric chair. He'd come within minutes of being executed for murder, only to be granted a stay of execution, and a new trial, at which he was subsequently acquitted. His many years behind prison walls had given him a tremendous craving for girls, and he was now realizing his dreams. With so much money and power and know-how, he was very attractive to them.

Louie's associates included Mel Ryan, who was tops in electronics, burglar alarms, and locks. He could wire up any kind of bomb and prevent even the best burglar alarms from tripping off. Mel was a high liver and traveled a great deal in his profession. Another friendly member was Bruce Conn, a tough ex-cop from back East. He'd been caught in some crooked activities and kicked off the police force. He was soon active in Louie's outfit, which took airplane trips like you'd go to the corner grocery.

Their specialty was robbing homes where large amounts of cash were kept. Generally, the jobs were fingered by close associates of the victims who had tax-free money hidden away. It was reported that on one job, they took off $150,000—cash.

Louie knew his trade well, was full of nerve, long on brawn, but short of brain power. However, those in his group looked up to him. While in the Federal Prison in Atlanta, he'd become close to Vito Genovese. When you're able to get close to Vito, you've got to carry the right credentials! The Police Gangster Squad probably knew this, too, for they kept him under heavy surveillance.

74

Louie started moving fast on the West Coast. Everyone was a little afraid of him. He had the smile of an angel and the sting of death. I often wondered how many men he'd really killed. He had knocked down quite a few rivals, and was regarded as an "ace" among hit men. And now he was starting to do things his own way; no advice from higher up. They warned him a few times about his erratic ways and questioned statements he'd made about some of the boys. In his group, there was always a little trouble in splitting up the money, and Louie always wound up with the biggest slice of the pie. He was slippery as an eel. His meetings were called either very late at night or early in the morning.

When Louie started stepping on too many of the boys, they called their own meeting and reached a verdict. A few weeks later, Louie was found parked in his big Cadillac, a bullet hole in his head. The police report read: "Gangland slaying. Open. Unsolved."

In the next few months, there was a little heat from the police on this slaying. But where could they look? And for whom? We all had so many enemies that none of us dared talk business in our cars for fear they'd been bugged. We'd either whisper, mouth our words, or use signs. Sometimes we'd park, get out, and move away from the cars to talk over our deals. We were living in the age of electronics, and it had the underworld in a sweat. When we'd get phone calls in our homes, it would be from pals in phone booths who'd give us a number to call. We'd have to drive to another booth to call their booth to find out what they wanted.

Eating in restaurants was no pleasure. You kept looking around—even under the tables—to see who was listening and if the place was bugged. We all talked in whispers, afraid to be overheard. Usually when we planned a meeting, we used a series of four or five different cars and kept switching to confuse the police. Sometimes we'd go into a building, out the back door and into another car to another place. Occasionally there would be helicopters tailing us in addition to the patrol cars.

Many in the underworld had legitimate businesses on the side. They muscled into a lot of big companies. Often this happened when big businessmen would contact people in the underworld when they needed help. As big as they were, they lacked the guts to get into anything violent. Perhaps a guy wanted to get rid of his partner. An underworld member would be hired to do him in or scare him so much he'd drop out of the business.

When the job was done, the hired man would be handed an envelope of money.

"Now the business is mine!" the executive would tell the underworld character.

"Is it?" would be his quiet answer.

This was known as "marrying the guy." The businessman would never be rid of his accomplice and would be blackmailed from then on.

All the crowd were heavy drinkers and avid gamblers. Some of the big guys had accumulated millions of dollars but were afraid to spend it. I wonder if Uncle Sam has any idea how much money is buried here and there by underworld members. But the vast majority didn't hang onto their cash for long. If you gamble, you have losses, and most of the addicts didn't know when to quit. I remember one heavy gambler who owed every bookie around, had lost his business, and was up against the wall. When one of our men went to collect from him, he said, "Do me a favor: kill me! My wife can collect the insurance."

Another way those in criminal activities lost a lot of money was that they were continually being brought to court on one count or another. Thousands of dollars went to bail bondsmen and lawyers and for fines. Tommy once said, "You know, the money we make isn't real. We're just working for the lawyers." They had us over a barrel. As we got older, we were not as sharp. We were running scared all the time.

Violence was always a part of our lives. I recall one incident that had its beginning at the Farmer's Market in Los Angeles. I enjoyed eating there. This tourist attraction catered to many movie celebrities who sought out its great variety of high-class food and interesting shops. The boys in the rackets always found it a relaxing place to eat the many delicacies at an outdoor table and eye the attractive girls. I knew many of the owners of the various businesses there, and at one time or another was involved with them, mainly through gambling and bookmaking. They were all good guys, and I did them some favors. If some pretty prostitute came to town, I'd fix it up with one of these men to be her Sugar Daddy during her stay. They were always good for a soft touch.

Rudy was one of the owners who had a thriving business and worked hard. He always looked up to me, and we were close for many years. Rudy loved to play the ponies and wanted more than anything to be one of the boys. For the last couple of years, bets on horses from his various clients would be called in to us, and we'd give him a percentage of the winnings at the end of the week. Then he'd bet his winnings with us and usually lose! He was a great guy, with a big heart, but he had very poor judgment.

His greeting to me was always "Hi, chief! Got any tips on the horses today?"

I'd always laugh. "Rudy, if you could beat the horses, race tracks and bookies would be out of action! Wake up, chum! Don't be a sucker. Don't bet on the horses. You can't win in the long run."

Now and then Rudy would get into scrapes with the guys and would call on me to help him. He trusted my judgment. One day, he introduced me to Terry Aldona. He seemed to be very impressed with this six-foot-four, handsome guy. Aldona wore the most expensive clothes and sported a $5,000 diamond ring on his little finger and flashed a $2,500 watch. He told me right away that he was a guy who knew all the angles.

As Aldona and I sat eating in a sunny area at the Market, we carried on a conversation about nothing, feeling each other out. I wanted to know why he was hanging around Rudy. I felt that, whatever his reason, my friend was going to wind up with the worst of it. As we talked, a few names were mentioned, and we found out we had some mutual friends. But we didn't exactly warm up to each other, and when I left, he seemed a little edgy to me.

I made some phone calls to check on this Terry Aldona among my pals in the underworld, but nobody knew him. So I tipped Rudy off to stay away from this flashy character. However, he didn't listen too well. I saw Terry several times after that at the Farmer's Market when I'd drop in to mix business with pleasure.

Finally, Terry suggested that Rudy buy a trailer load of hot merchandise. Rudy came to me greatly elated. He suggested I buy the stuff, and divide the profits with him. He said Terry wanted to talk to me about the deal. Although I didn't like the smell of it, I met with Terry and let him do all the talking. Something didn't jell with this guy. I said nothing other than that I'd think it over.

In the next few days, I did some more checking on him and learned his real name was not Terry Aldona, but Terri Mazzo, and he was suspected of being the trigger-man in a recent killing. A few years before, he had been in a "Social Group of Hijackers" who'd been caught. Terri had been suspected of making a deal with the cops, because he was the only one of the group to be set free. He had left the East in a big hurry and had seemingly decided to set up business in Los Angeles.

I contacted Terri and turned him down cold. From then on, he became scarce at the Farmer's Market. But one day Rudy had a visit from the FBI. It seems that Terri had been using Rudy's business phones to call his friends in a hot car racket, then they'd call back and reverse the charges. All this was unknown to Rudy, but the FBI had been able to trace the calls. Naturally, he was suspected of being involved. After weeks of visits from the Feds and the intense questioning of all of Rudy's associates, he was asked to vacate his business at the Market. He was ruined. I felt sorry for the guy. Terri had gotten him into this mess, and then had disappeared.

But several weeks later, Terri got his. One morning, he got into his expensive sports car with his little boy and noticed a small box under the front seat. Like the rest of us in the criminal world, he was always wary. The box had some small antennae attached to it, so he assumed it was a police bug. These devices are rather common, and can transmit conversations in the car to cops some distance away. Terri picked it up gently, examined it carefully, then placed it back under the seat. Instead of driving away then, he returned to his swanky home and phoned his friend Carmen to tell him what he'd found. The friend wanted to see it, so he and the boy drove over to let him examine the contraption. They both agreed it was a police bug, but they returned it to the car. Terri's son stayed at the friend's home, and the two men left to take care of some business. Carmen was a bit of a rounder and hustler, and they were in on some deals together.

Before they had driven very far, there was a tremendous explosion. The box hadn't been a police bug after all, but a cleverly devised remote-control bomb. Some men in a car that had been following Terri had waited until the small son had left, then set off the bomb under the seat by radio impulse. Terri's head was blown off, and Carmen was hurled through the roof of the convertible. He landed twenty feet away. By a miracle, he survived, which is how we eventually learned the details of what happened. The headlines read: GANGLAND REPRISAL SLAYING.

Today, the underworld has some of the best men in electronics. Cars always have to be checked very carefully inside and out. It's no longer just a matter of a bomb wired under the hood and connected to the starter. And if it isn't the underworld geniuses rigging up your car, it's the police and their clever electronic devices. They can not only pick up your conversations, but can trace your route of travel.

We never knew, when we woke up each morning, if we'd live till night. Criminals are unpredictable, and we were constantly apprehensive, wondering if we'd been set up for a kill. More and more of my pals were being murdered. There was Willie Alvarado, one of my oldest friends. He was starting to go back on his word and knew he was walking on thin ice. I met him one day to talk over his problems. A few days later, he was found in his parked car, shot dead.

We knew we didn't have any true friends. All you could trust was your gun and the money in your pocket. Every time someone close to me met a violent death, I was one of the first the police picked up as a suspect. I had been getting away with a lot, and the police wanted to pin something on me. The heat was really on.

8

One morning, I had breakfast with Vince and The Greek. At this point, Vince was taking care of my business. I told him I had to get away from the pressure of Los Angeles and had decided to fly East for a vacation. Maybe the police would be cooled off by the time I returned. Before we parted, The Greek had thought up a scheme where we could make twenty grand, and I gave him my okay.

It was good to be away from California and to see new territory. I visited my mom in Pennsylvania and lived it up in some of the Eastern cities before returning to L.A. three weeks later.

As my plane approached the L.A. airport, I was acutely aware of that strange empty feeling inside me. I thought, Well, here you are; going right back to the same old rat race!

The Greek picked me up in his Cadillac, and we went to his swank penthouse apartment to talk about our latest business deal. He had reported to me when I was away that it had gone over real good. Now that I was back, he didn't dig up my share. Said he'd lost it at the racetrack.

I was furious! I went to his kitchen, grabbed a butcher knife, and putting it to his throat, knocked him violently against the wall. As we stood there, high above the street, he pleaded, "Don't do this to me!"

I whispered, "You can swindle all your jellyfish friends, but you can't do it to me."

I wanted to throw him out the window. Then I looked at him—handsome, suave, intelligent—and I realized I needed him. We had other deals going, and he had a lot of know-how and nerve. It was too bad he had to play the horses. He'd made and lost millions, and he and I would make plenty again. So I decided I'd kill him later. For the present, he was valuable to me.

The perspiration was running off his chin as we faced each other by the window. I lowered the butcher knife from his throat and shoved him back into the corner. He sank onto a sofa, exhausted with fear. He had to recover, so for the next week he relaxed at Palm Springs. It was one of his favorite spots, where he could mingle with movie and society people and conduct a few con games.

That night, I came home and went into my old routine of arguing with my wife. She hardly saw me anymore, but when she did, she had to listen to filthy language and loud curses. When she'd tell me she was worried about the life I was living, I'd slap her hard and tell her not to meddle in my affairs.

I got away the next morning to fish at Catalina. It was a perfect day for catching fish. The air was clear, and I felt alive and good. I had to be alone like this to think clearly, especially now since I was planning a scheme that involved big money. It was important that I avoid taking chances; I didn't want to go to jail again.

One of the schemes I was in on concerned the racetrack. We had noted that sometimes races would start a few minutes earlier than the time announced if the weather was bad or the crowds small. I'd be at the track and would get a call in a phone booth at a prearranged time. I'd put in a big bet on the race, being careful because the booths are sometimes monitored. I'd give the name of the horse in code: a horse that had just run and won. A few minutes made a lot of difference.

We had fantastic things going—until the San Diego police got wise to it, and two of my pals and I were hauled off to jail. One of us, Frankie, had $1,800 stashed in his shoes, and my other pal had $800 on him, so the trusties in the jail were good to us and we weren't there long.

Now and then, I'd run into Tommy, my old pal from the early days in the rackets. He had branched out in his own bookmaking empire in California and had made it big. He lived in an estate area in Toluca Lake in the Valley with a girl named Shirley, who knew as much about bookmaking as we did. Occasionally, Tommy and I would give each other a piece of the winnings if we won a lot of money on a horse.

I'd always like Tommy. He was kind and to my knowledge had never been involved in violence. He was a good businessman, but he was really living it up. Often we'd sit and chat in a restaurant over a cup of coffee.

"Joe, the more money I make, the quicker it goes," Tommy would remark in his Okie drawl. "I wish I could be like you and stay away from gambling. One of these days, I'm going to go legit and pack the rackets in!"

I saw him one day when he'd just come off a $100,000 con game score from a guy he'd taken as a partner. He also told me about his new flame, Hilda. He described her as a beautiful, intelligent girl, and said she was keeping his books. He acted nervous and seemed worried, and when I mentioned it, he admitted he was afraid he was being followed.

He was right. A week later, Tommy's whole operation was busted. He and his workers had been tailed for months. Tommy had a bad habit of slipping every once in a while on the telephones, and they'd been tapped for quite a while. Tommy, Hilda, and many of the people who worked for him were indicted. The girl was found guilty but released on bail pending sentencing. Tommy faced trial and prison.

Shortly after this, Tommy and Hilda were having dinner at an exclusive restaurant. Those at adjacent tables couldn't help but overhear their noisy argument. Hilda was in tears. They left hurriedly, and in the parking lot the attendants were aware of their continued angry words. Tommy got in on the passenger's side, expecting Hilda to drive. She opened the car door, reached into her purse, and drew out a .38 revolver. She pointed the weapon at Tommy and pulled the trigger three times. Bullets hit him in the chest, the shoulder, and the head. Then, with tears streaming from her eyes, she placed the revolver to her own head and pulled the trigger a fourth time.

My other lieutenant, Bloomie, and I went to the viewing in the Slumber Room at the mortuary.

"You can't get used to death, nohow!" Bloomie said. "Gee, Tommy looks sad. Oh, well, he's out of his misery."

"Yeah," I agreed. "And he doesn't have to worry about going to jail anymore."

Bloomie thought for a moment, then took two racetrack tickets and stuck them in Tommy's pocket.

"Maybe they'll have a track where he's going," he explained.

Bloomie and I were followed to Tommy's funeral. The police had a zoom camera at the cemetery, and took pictures of all who attended the service. The underworld was well represented. When we left the funeral, two plainclothes detectives tailed us and pulled our car over to the curb. They made us get out with our hands above our heads, and they searched the car and us. It was just a routine police roust, and we'd been through it many times before. They let us go, but we were burned up over the way they had ruined Tommy's funeral.

A few months later, I got some information about a fixed horse race. My pals and I bet a pretty amount of money on that horse with most of the local bookies. The horse won, of course, and paid a big price. The incident created quite a bit of flurry around California. I was called before the Federal Grand Jury on two different occasions because of this racket. We all took the Fifth Amendment and refused to answer the questions. A few of my associates wound up in jail, but I was spared an indictment in this case.

One of our big shots, Saldi, thought I had what it takes to move up in the underworld. He knew I'd been wanting to get out of the heat in Los Angeles, so he told me to contact a guy named Dominic in Pennsylvania. It was a chance at a top job—and with the mob's blessings. Saldi said there were two musclemen standing in the way of his activities back there, and I had the right qualifications to get them straightened out.

I flew back to meet Dominic in Reading. Before I'd been there forty-eight hours, the police knew I was in town, and I figured I'd better give up the whole plan. I wouldn't stand a chance with John Habecker, the Chief of Detectives, breathing down my neck. So I came back to Los Angeles with its same old rackets, same old dangers—and my same old miserable family.

Shortly after I got back, I received a long-distance call from Mr. Cigaro. As usual, I went out to a pay phone and called him back. Cigaro had some plans and was calling for a meeting with Boom Boom, The Kid and me. The following week, we took a trip and met Mr. Cigaro. He'd arrived an hour early, as was his habit, to look everything over. When we got there, Mr. Cigaro asked the questions, gave the answers, and there were no objections.

The meeting had been called to discuss Andy, who had a key position in the gambling field. We'd been trying to get control of a part of his interests so we could be in a position to dictate to the bookies and people in the gambling business. Andy had the key in the wire service. But it had been rumored that he was also a police informer. We discussed his activities and the power we could wield if we had his business.

The Kid kept remarking, "I don't trust the blankety-blank Irishman!"

I suggested we take him for a ride.

"But we need him," Boom Boom said. "You can't kill everybody."

As always, Mr. Cigaro made the final decision. "Scare him to death! You pick the method."

We first considered a bomb with only enough force to blow the hood off his car. That would scare anybody. However, Andy was very careful where he parked his Cadillac, so we ruled that out.

About a week later, Andy and two of his associates were in his business establishment when a car drove by and an automatic rifle sprayed the large plate-glass windows of the building. Everyone inside dove to the floor. As the men in the car drove away, they had a big laugh. Later, the shell casings on the floor of the car were cleaned out. We made sure there was no evidence tying us in with this piece of work.

Andy reached out for help after that, and a meeting was arranged between him and myself. Always leery of any confab, I staked myself out to watch Andy's establishment the night before our meeting. After I'd been in hiding an hour, I saw Andy and two husky men carrying what appeared to be electronic equipment into the meeting place. It didn't take an Einstein to figure out that Andy was setting me up to get all our conversation on tape for the police. I called Mr. Cigaro and told him what I had seen. We agreed that I should go to the meeting and reverse the conversation. This was to be a joke on Andy, the informer.

At ten o'clock the next morning, I kept our appointment. Andy's face looked pale and worn. He forced a smile, then showed me the bullet holes. He confided that he was afraid for his life. There had even been threatening phone calls, he said. He was more than ready to make a deal with the people I was associated with.

In the back of my mind, I kept thinking, "This rat must really believe I'm a donkey!" I could imagine all this conversation going onto a beautiful tape to be played before a Grand Jury or a packed courtroom.

After Andy had finished complaining, he waited for me to bury myself with some incriminating remarks.

I said, "Andy, you've really got my sympathy. But it sounds to me more like you've been running around with some guy's wife, and he's the one who riddled this building."

Andy looked stunned. Before he could open his mouth, I told him, "Andy, you've got more enemies than you realize. It's going around that you've been robbing many bookies by working into their organizations and swindling people out of their profits."

His jaw dropped. "What do you mean?"

"Listen, the longer I look at those bullet holes, the more I realize this is a dangerous place just to be in! I don't want to get involved with you." I rose to leave. "You're a crook, and I've got a wife and two kids. I'm getting out of here before your enemies come back."

Andy yelled, "Hey, wait a minute! I want to make a deal! I'm scared."

I walked toward the door. "Andy, I don't know what you're talking about. Goodbye—and good luck!"

As an afterthought, I turned and said, "By the way, you look terrible! I'd call the police if I were you; it might have been one of those crazy snipers!"

I got into my car feeling very smug and satisfied. Andy had tried to set me up, but it had backfired. I saw him a few months later. He looked like a walking dead man. Twice he glanced over his shoulder like he was scared of being followed. Over the next couple of years, he was continually looking for a gangland reprisal.

9

After my return to Los Angeles, I was soon back in the usual round of parties, often staying out all night, then going home to change clothes. Like the rest of the boys, I had a spare apartment for partying. But I did have to go home now and then.

My wife tried hard to run a good home and live a decent life. Ours was a modest home in a quiet neighborhood in Burbank. Unlike most of my underworld pals, I avoided putting up a big front. The Internal Revenue men watch the guys who live lavishly.

Living modestly was easy for Jean, who had been brought up in a poor family. She was naturally frugal and always shopped for bargains. I had to force her to buy new clothes. She'd tell me she wanted to save money, because she never knew when something might happen to me and she'd be left alone to raise our kids.

She was clever with her hands and molded beautiful things out of papier-mâché. She had to keep her hands and mind occupied to blank out her frustrations over me and my way of life. Being active in PTA and Girl Scout work, she made some good friends, but I discouraged her from asking anyone to our home. For a while, she helped to edit the school paper, and my daughter was very proud of her. Except to my circle of friends, Jean was very outgoing and wanted to have closer relationships with the women she met.

"There are real people out there in the world," she said to me one day, "but you don't know them."

"They're all a bunch of phonies," I jeered. "Your only true friend is a dollar bill."

Sometimes she would fall to her knees and scream, "Why? Why? We have these two wonderful kids, and we could have such a happy life." Whenever she pulled this, I'd get angrier than ever, feeling that she was just being weak.

How many times she begged me, "Joe, please give us some kind of life! I worry every second. These kids need a father!"

She'd throw herself on the floor, like a child having a tantrum, and cry, "Oh, dear God, I wish I was dead!"

But she never got any sympathy from me. "Oh, shut up, will you! You drive me nuts," I'd sneer. "I give you money. What more do you want, you blankety-blank broad!"

The arguments would go on and on, growing louder and more furious. Then my hands would come down on her face or into her stomach. And this went on for years and years.

I shouldn't have been surprised when she took off with the kids for Salt Lake City where her mother lived. I was sure she was gone for good, for our last fights had really been fierce. I sent all their clothes after them, and I even wired her to pick up her "mangy cat" which I'd put on a plane.

With my family gone, I felt completely free. For a

while, my home was the new place for partying. I could invite my pals and my fancy women over, and we'd really swing.

I was still busy with my various illegal activities, and time seemed to fly. I heard that Jean was working at a part-time job in Utah and evidently was satisfied with our separation. Within a year, I was served some papers. She'd started divorce proceedings in Salt Lake City.

Suddenly, I really felt empty. The home had become just a house. Parties began to seem dull and disgusting. I needed my Jeanie—more than ever before. One night I phoned her and asked her to come back; I told her that her place was with me. After a long talk, she decided to forget about the divorce. She came back, but reminded me it was only so the kids could have a father.

Soon, we were all together again, but I kept on with my old tricks.

Our gang was enraged over a union dispute—a case where the workers had been out on a long strike. We decided to launch a statewide stink-bomb campaign in sympathy. Boom Boom and I and a few others got ahold of a lot of potent little plastic bottles filled with a substance that outsmelled any skunk. We'd go into a building, lay one down in an inconspicuous place, pull the cap, and get out fast. Once we emptied out a packed theater. The police could never pin it on anyone.

But our campaign backfired. We began to have accidents with the bombs and got the vile-smelling stuff on our clothes and hands. We'd have to lay low for a week. Some of our cars really reeked. My wife couldn't understand why I smelled to high heaven. I finally had to throw away my clothes. One of the guys, a bartender, couldn't go to work. Another pal had his contaminated shoes on his outside windowsill until all the neighbors complained. The whole campaign fizzled out before it had hardly begun.

It was only a matter of weeks before Jean's and my

arguments were as violent as ever. Nothing had changed, and, if possible, things seemed to be getting even worse. About this time, in March of '71, my brother Tony and his family decided to visit their relatives in Los Angeles. It was their first trip, and I was eager to show them the sights. I got up very early one morning while Jean and the kids were still asleep, and drove to the airport to meet them. As I left the house, I had a strange feeling something was wrong. Jean usually would stir and tell me goodbye when I left early. I decided she was still angry over our last violent argument.

I picked up Tony and his family and brought them back to my home. They loved every mile of the drive, marveling at the great city and the beautiful scenery. We were all laughing and joking as we entered the house. Jean's car was in the driveway, and I was glad she'd be there to greet our guests.

The house was ominously still. We stood for a moment, listening for some greeting. Then, suddenly, my little boy staggered into the room and fell at my feet. I picked him up, and he fell again! About that time, my daughter appeared from her bedroom, reeling as if she were drunk. She swayed to one side and fell against a chair. We all stood there, shocked, not believing our eyes. As I knelt beside them, they muttered faintly, "Mommy, mommy—"

"What about mommy?" I asked urgently.

"Pills."

I ran into our bedroom. She was still breathing! We rushed the three of them to the hospital.

Jean—poor, wretched, and desperate—had finally given up. She had taken God-only-knows-how-many sleeping pills and given some to John and Karen. For the first time, I blamed myself for something. I looked back over all the violence and frustration she had lived through being my wife, and I knew I had driven her to this horrible act. It was all my fault.

I made a maximum effort, then, to start being the husband and father I should have been all along. And for a while it looked like I was really changed.

10

Things had been peaceful around the house for several months, actually, and then one noon, Jean and I had a violent argument. I slapped her, knocked her down, and threatened to kill her. She ran out of the house, screaming.

That night, she left. I said to myself, "Good riddance! I'll get along. John and Karen won't be hard to take care of. We'll be all right."

But I had never known what a job it was, raising a twelve-year-old girl and a ten-year old boy. I'd always left it all up to Jean. All those meals, those dirty clothes, the dirty house, the marketing, taking the kids to school—I did my best, but it was woefully short of what was needed.

Worst of all, the kids missed their mother terribly, and were looking to me for some kind of love and affection. But I didn't even know what it was. "Oh, God," I pleaded one night, in absolute desperation, "I can't do it! I'm phony, empty, nothing. If You're there, listen to me! Let Jesus come into my heart!" Where were the words coming from? I didn't know what I was saying.

Nothing happened, of course, but the next day the thought came to me to call my mother. "Ma, you got to come out here and help me with these kids. I really need you bad."

"Joe, you know I've been real sick, and I'm still sick. They want to operate on my spine to release the pressure on the nerves, the pain is so bad. I can't work, I can't do anything."

I knew that she was, if anything, understating it, because my mother never showed her pain or suffering to anyone. "Ma, I'm sorry I called. I just didn't know where else to turn."

"Well, I'll pray for you, and we'll see."

Within three days, she called back. A miracle had happened. She could walk and move without pain, and she was making arrangements to come West as soon as possible. In three more days, she was there.

But I couldn't settle down to my old routine. The terrible nightmares began again, when I'd finally drop off to sleep. Every night, I took sleeping pills, and by day I popped tranquilizers. Marijuana and alcohol did nothing for me. I even started going to a class on hypnosis, but nothing helped.

One day, in connection with one of our schemes, a power cable as thick as a woman's wrist had to be cut. My associates were scared to death of electricity, and so was I. But I had to prove myself, so I nominated myself for the job. I'd committed almost every kind of crime, but still felt I had to show the guys how absolutely without fear I was.

The job had to be done, and the night was picked. I pulled on the thick rubber gloves and started to saw through the huge cable, watching in terror as the sparks leaped out, turning the sawblade black. I tried to stop.

But some strange force kept my arm moving in a sawing motion. I couldn't help myself.

There was no sleep for me for weeks afterward. I had had my first run-in with raw, naked evil, and I knew it was all too real.

One day, after meeting with the boys and receiving my envelope of money for my week's take of our gambling business, I played some handball at the YMCA. I played to relax, to relieve my churning mind. At this time, I was deeply involved in the con games using my different voices. Thousands of dollars were involved. We thought we had a good thing going for us, but it had me tied up in knots.

The Greek, Vince, and I parted that day with our pockets full of money. But as I drove home, I felt more empty than I had ever felt before in my life. I was a dead man, walking around standing up.

That evening, I went to my hypnotism class, and the doctor talked to someone in the spirit world. This impressed me, but made me more confused than ever. The teacher's theory was that, when we die, our spirit is put in another body, and we come back. I thought, "That's a joke!" In the class were people from all walks of life, including some from the movie and television industries. They were all seeking the same answer I was. Something was missing in their lives; they didn't know what it was.

I had met a girl after a few weeks of these sessions, and we were attracted to each other. Marie was an intelligent, attractive person who worked for a large recording company in Hollywood. That night, we went out for a few drinks and ended up at her apartment. I had been dating her for some time, and after the class the previous week, I had spent the night with her and a bottle of booze. It had been great while it lasted, but as I drove home, I felt lonelier than ever. The emptiness inside me had grown bigger than I was.

Yet there I was again with this beautiful girl who did

her best to entertain me. That night, she, too, admitted she was searching for something. She knew the same emptiness inside. This love affair wasn't the answer for either of us, and, earlier than I had anticipated, I headed for home.

Going into the house, I prepared for bed. I expected the same old routine: another sleepless night, interspersed with a few nightmares when I finally did doze off. The house was still. I checked the doors and windows to make sure everything was secure. The light was on in front of the house, and I switched on the one in the rear. I laid my head on the pillow, and tried relaxing and talking myself to sleep, which was part of the hypnosis exercise I'd been learning. It hadn't worked before, but I was still trying. I had been needing tranquilizers to get any rest for my mind, but that night, I didn't take any

Even so, I went into a sound sleep. Awakening, I noticed the bedside clock read seven o'clock. Seven! Where had the night gone? There had been no tossing or fighting for sleep, no frightening dreams. I hadn't slept like that for years. I felt so rested and relaxed.

It was time to get up and get things going, with my mother's help. There was the kids' breakfast, and Johnny's lunch to pack. I sat on the edge of the bed, searching with bare feet for my slippers.

The next thing I knew, I was standing straight up, lifted there by something, or Someone. And I felt something in the room. Something—was there. The word *God* seemed to go right through my heart. God. God.

My first thought was, "Oh my God, oh my God. There is a God." The presence in the room became stronger—it was beautiful. Perfect. Love. "Oh, God, oh God, oh God," I murmured.

It was so beautiful, I thought my heart would burst. God was *real!* He was *alive!* I'd always thought He was just a word, for weak people who needed a crutch, for old women—but now He was here, in this room!

97

The presence continued to build. It was unbearable—I couldn't stand it, but I wanted more. And the presence came right inside of me, into my heart. And filled it. With love.

I'd heard that just before you die, you feel good, and I figured that was what was happening to me. I was about to die. God had come to kill me for the bad things I'd done.

I looked over at my little boy, lying there on his bed, and said, "God, You can kill me. I know I deserve it, but who's going to watch after the children?"

Then God seemed to touch me again, and I felt like I was rising up through the air. And the beautiful voice of God, inside of me, but all around me, too, said, *You're reborn*. It sounded like loudspeakers, but so soft— *You're reborn, you're reborn,* over and over, off the walls, off the ceiling, off my heart. I could hear nothing but this beautiful soft voice.

This is so wonderful, I kept thinking, but I still wondered if I was going to die and this was a foretaste of paradise. And then the Lord said in the same still, soft voice: *Tell your friends.* So—He wanted me to stay. Yes, I found myself nodding, yes, yes, yes.

I ran into the kitchen to prepare breakfast, running because I wanted to feel the firmness of the floor beneath me, to make sure I wasn't traveling around a couple of inches up in the air. The meal seemed to prepare itself! I began to sing. Heaven was around me, inside me, throughout my spirit.

My mother and the children came into the kitchen and stared at me while I sang, setting the table.

"You all look wonderful today," I told them over and over again.

Glancing at the morning paper, I read the dateline aloud, "Wednesday March 8, 1972." What a day to be reborn. As I ate, I realized the food had never tasted better. I was a new human being in a new world. All I felt was love, joy, and peace. The emptiness was gone. God had filled that hollow space deep inside me. Wow! It was all so beautiful. "God came to me," I kept saying to myself.

I took the children to school, and the car seemed to be floating, too. After dropping them off and telling them I loved them—which was a rare speech for me—I returned home. I still couldn't fully comprehend what was happening, but I felt immersed in a heavenly feeling as if the hand of God was on me. I was loving every precious second of this born-again experience.

I walked around the house looking at everything as if for the first time. In the backyard, everything was more beautiful than I could believe. The birds sang louder; the grass was greener; the sky bluer. My life was full and whole, and I was forgiven for every wrong I had ever done. And I knew it!

After I'd showered and dressed for the day, I jumped into my car and turned on the ignition and the radio. For some reason, my favorite rock station wouldn't come on Something took my eye to the radio dial. As I watched, it moved to another station! I'd had an expensive new FM radio and tape deck installed a week before, but obviously something wasn't working right. I moved the dial back to the rock station. Again the dial turned itself to another station. I couldn't believe what was happening. I turned it back again to the rock program, but before the wild music could even start, the dial again turned by itself to 99.5 FM!

On this station, there was a religious program, and the speakers were talking about Jesus, loud and clear. Everything they said was being drawn into my heart, mind, and soul. I drove onto the freeway, listening, digesting every word of the Good News of Jesus Christ over a radio station I'd never heard of before. The music was beautiful. "The Old Rugged Cross," "What a Friend We Have in Jesus" . . . so many wonderful songs! I began to hum along with them as I drove down the freeway.

I exclaimed, "Oh God, I am so happy! I'm free. The chains of the world and its problems have snapped. I've found everything I ever wanted—and much more! If I could put this into a bottle or pill, the whole world could be changed in one minute!"

At the dinner table that night, we listened to the religious station. Every radio in the house was tuned in to 99.5 FM. I was learning about the Bible, and I knew that every word of it was true. A few months earlier, if you'd asked me who Jesus was, I would likely have cracked, "Where does He tend bar?" or "What football team does He quarterback for?" Now I was loving everything I heard about Him, and I was hungry to learn more.

That night, I had another heavenly sleep. No nightmares, just peace, rest, and joy. I jumped out of bed early the next morning, glad to be alive. Before this, I'd hated to get up and face the world.

God took me to the backyard. I couldn't see Him, but His Spirit led me. I stood under an avocado tree and prayed. Then something happened. It was as if He reached down and lifted me right up out of myself. Suddenly, everything looked different, as if washed by the water of heaven. I thought, Oh God, this is a taste of heaven! It's so, so beautiful! I want this forever.

As I seemed to come back down, I thought, Oh, God, I don't want to see anybody go to hell. The Lord seemed to tell me, *Walk with Me*. And I made up my mind to do just that.

All that day I was singing. As I rode in my car, my ears were glued constantly to the FM station teaching about Jesus. Suddenly the thought came to me that maybe I'd died two days before and was only a heavenly spirit on earth. But no, I'd taken the kids to school, I'd eaten breakfast, I was driving my car. Yet it seemed as if I was riding on air with God beside me. I felt that I was a direct part of God, like His son in the flesh.

I know this all sounds strange. But words can never describe the experience I was having. It was too magnificent for human expression.

When the family gathered at mealtime, I'd tell them about Jesus returning soon, about His love for us, and how He'd died for our sins. They listened, puzzled. Was this Joe? The same daddy whose nerves were shattered, speaking without any tension, anger, or foul language? They couldn't figure out what was happening.

I postponed my appointments with my underworld associates with one excuse after another. I wanted to stay close to the radio and learn all I could about this wonderful experience I was having. Furthermore, I was trying to figure out how to tell my friends about God's message. He had told me through His Spirit, *Tell your friends,* and I knew He meant the underworld and the Mafia especially.

The third night, I again went into a deep, sound, secure sleep. I awakened eagerly in the morning, sensing that something beautiful was soon going to happen. I started my day with a prayer, then went into the daily routine. As I took my kids to school, I found myself singing and praising God. I told the kids how much I loved them, and they were happy—if confused—about the change in their dad.

Alone in my car, I experienced another miracle. I felt God there in the car, and the heavens rang with the words, *Touch and heal.* I wanted to run down the street and touch every sick person I could find and watch God heal them. It was incredible. And I knew in my heart that I would see people made whole and that it would be in *His* time and *His* way.

I called the doctor who conducted the hypnotism classes and made an appointment. This Jewish gentleman listened to me in his office, but couldn't fathom what I was saying. He admitted I had a light in my face and eyes that hadn't been there before, but he tried to

101

convince me it was the result of his teachings in hypnosis. He was grasping for some kind of logic and not coming up with the right answers.

I had to find those answers myself. At home again, I hunted up my daughter's large Bible and began to read it. I was hungry to know every word, and God made it all clear. It wasn't long before I was looking for a church. There were ten close to me, but God directed me to the Valley Community Church in Burbank. There were only twenty-five people in the little church the night I went. I talked to Pastor Keller, telling him what had happened to me, and he explained that I was a born-again Christian and a member of God's family. He had me tell the congregation about my life and my background. When the service was over, many of them hugged and even kissed me! Perfect strangers!

I finally met with the boys a few days later. They remarked about how different I looked. Vince said, "Joe, you're glowing with joy! Are you taking some kind of special pills?"

When the meeting broke up, I was handed the usual envelope of money. I felt it was dirty and said to myself that I would use it for some worthy cause. There were so many. Already I was enumerating them in my mind: the poor, the ex-prisoners and ex-addicts—who need so much help and encouragement.

For the next few weeks, I saw my friends as little as possible. When I did run into any of them, I would turn the conversation to Jesus, the Bible, and God.

One evening, I had a date with Marie. We had some drinks but they didn't affect me. I tried marijuana with her but couldn't get high. Then I realized I didn't need these things anymore. I was elevated with God. I could feel Jesus telling me that liquor and marijuana were wrong, and I found myself telling Marie about the Bible and Christ's return.

"Joe," she said, looking at me, "you won't be seeing

102

me again. I know it."

And at that moment, I felt a sharp kick at my leg—though she was several feet away. I knew it was God's way of saying, *Joe, get out of here.* And that was the last time I saw Marie.

The following day, I met with my associates in a restaurant. They politely inquired about the "Jesus kick" I was on, halfheartedly smiling. I took their sarcasm for a while, then came right out with it. I blurted out, "Jesus came to me in my bedroom. I'm born again! And He told me to tell all you guys."

Then, as God gave me strength, I told them nearly all that had been happening to me. I also told them that what they were doing was wrong.

"Fellas, you're on your way to hell! Ask Jesus to forgive your sins and to come into your hearts."

Spoons and cups dropped heavily onto the table. I thought The Greek was going to choke! Vince was shaking his head in disbelief. They were speechless. Was this the cold-blooded, crazy, cunning Joe they knew?

They gave me my envelope of money and left in silence.

By the time I got home, the phone was ringing. It was my brother Ralph. "What's all this Jesus thing about?"

"Ralph, it's all true. He came to me in my bedroom, and—"

"I heard it already. All the boys in Southern California are talking about it. Listen, Joe—a little religion is all right, but you're too strong in this Jesus thing."

We talked for a long time, then later I went to his home with a Bible in my hand. Wow! That did it. But when I had a Bible in my hand, I felt more secure than with all the guns I'd carried in that other life.

Why had such extraordinary supernatural experiences happened to me? I believe I know. I had lived such a violent life, breaking every moral and civil law, that God had to wake me up and make me *know* it was Him.

103

Pastor Keller counseled me more than once: "Joe, God is going to use you, *if* you'll let Him guide every step of your Christian walk. Live only for God, and you'll have the most beautiful and rewarding life imaginable." I loved this brother for what he was teaching me. He even came over to my house in his spare time.

One of the things he taught me was that God had commanded believers to be baptized—to be completely immersed under water. A date was set for the baptismal service in his small church, and two weeks later, my boy John, a six-year-old girl, and I were baptized in the name of the Father, the Son, and the Holy Ghost.

11

At this time, I was still personally involved in many things with the gang and making lots of money. My brain, wits, and voice were needed in our operations. Vince and The Greek pleaded with me to finish with our business deals and not let them hang in the air until they could get reorganized without me. They somehow sensed I would never put any of them behind bars with what I knew about their criminal activities. And, to this day, they've been right about that.

Several years ago, Jim Vaus, another member of the underworld, had an experience similar to mine. Deeply involved with crime—mainly wiretapping—Jim was with a well-known mobster in California. Then one day, his whole life changed when he accepted Christ into his heart. When he went back into the underworld and told all his friends what had happened to him, they thought he was crazy, and they planned to kill him. But God had His protective hand on Jim who eventually went into evangelistic work with Billy Graham. However, he brought no harm on his friends by squealing on them. Instead, he went back to tell them about Jesus. Many of them learned to respect him and the work he was doing. Some of his old pals are still close to him.

Jim had cushioned the shock of Joe Donato's sudden change.

Vince met me several times alone, observing every motion I made and every word I spoke. "Joe, I know something happened to you. You look different, like deep down you're really happy."

Every time I'd see him, he'd try to persuade me to stay with the gang for a while and use my end of the take for church work. He had me thinking seriously about this for several weeks. Would it be okay to take dirty money and use it in prison evangelism and youth work? I felt that Christ was coming soon, and I needed to move fast to get the word of salvation to everyone I could.

But one day when Vince handed me my share of the money, the Spirit of God came upon me with conviction: *If you walk with God, you can't keep one foot in the world's darkness.* That was the last envelope. I sent the money to KHOF in Glendale, California, for their radio and television ministry. This Christian station was telling me and thousands of others about this man Jesus. I listened to it constantly.

For a while, I continued attending the hypnotism classes, thinking that this might be a way to get to know God better. But the instructor resented my increasing references to God and His power, particularly when the people in the class began to take a real interest in what had happened to me.

One night, he had had it. Without asking me, he said to the class, "Tonight, we're going to put Joe's newfound faith to the test."

He called me forward, and having no idea what he had in his mind, I went, praying that God would be with me,

106

and would use the test, whatever it was.

"First," said the instructor, "we'll demonstrate the power of hypnosis and automatic suggestion. I'm going to take this flame—" He produced a butane lighter, and turned the flame all the way up, till it reached about four inches. "Now I'll pass it under Joe's hand, and he will feel no pain." He turned to me. "Extend your left hand, palm down."

I did as he asked, and he started to intone, "Your hand is growing numb. All feeling is leaving it. It is—"

"Oh, God, protect me," I prayed, paying no attention to the instructor. At length, he brought the lighter under my palm, waving it back and forth close to my palm. I couldn't bear to look, so I shut my eyes, but I felt only a distant warmth on my hand. "Thank You, God," I prayed, as the instructor, well-pleased, was giving hypnosis the credit.

"Now," he said grimly, "we'll test the right hand without hypnosis. He will not be able to stand the heat and will pull his hand away."

"Oh, God," I prayed. "No pain, no pain!" And I chuckled then, because in my heart I knew there wouldn't be any. My chuckle seemed to goad the instructor on.

"Now watch as he pulls his hand away from the searing heat," he said, fiendishly thrusting the lighter right under my right palm and holding it there. The class gasped, and several of the women cried out and buried their heads in their hands.

"No pain, God. No pain!" I laughed out loud, because there wasn't any, not even the faint warmth I had felt before. Quietly furious, the instructor stuck the flame between my fingers, making sure the hottest part of the flame was touching my flesh. There still wasn't any pain.

"What do you think you're trying to pull?" he hissed under his breath to me, and I just laughed the harder.

Then the instructor tried to laugh, too, and make light

107

of it. But he was visibly shaken. And I knew that hypnosis was a poor counterfeit of God's power.

The class came up to examine my hands. Not one hair had been singed on the right, although the flame had been kept there three times longer than on the left. I knew I'd been under the protection of God.

At this time, I was really concerned about my boy John. He had a high fever that just wouldn't let go, no matter what my mother did. After three days, I went to Pastor Keller's church and shared my concern with the people there. The elders anointed a handkerchief with oil, prayed over it, and then gave it to me.

I took the cloth home, and when I got there, I laid it on John's chest while he dozed fitfully. Then, thinking of the Lord's promise that I would one day touch and heal, I laid my hands on him and prayed. Nothing happened.

Disappointed, I went to bed that night in his room. About 2:00 A.M., I awakened sharply, not knowing why. It was dark in the room, but I could make out the outline of the furniture in the room from the little moonlight that came in on either side of the window shade.

For some reason, I looked out the bedroom door and up the hall. Suddenly I saw a light about the size of a basketball coming down the hall toward the bedroom. It seemed to be swirling erratically as it came, and it was white, like starlight.

As it came closer, I was terrified and started to put my hands up in front of my face. The moment I did, the light disappeared, and at that moment my son sat up in his bed and put his arms up. "Daddy!" he shouted. "I'm healed. I'm all well!"

So God *did* hear my prayers and did honor the prayer cloth! In His way, and in His time. I wanted to get out of bed and thank Him on my knees, but I was still shaking like a leaf from what I had seen. So I did my praying staring wide-eyed at the ceiling.

The next morning, John jumped from his bed as good

as new without a sign of sickness. What zip, what sparkle he had! He didn't remember a thing from the night before.

One night shortly after that, John and I were attending church. In the middle of the service, he grabbed my hand tightly, and I felt a great presence of the Lord.

"It happened, daddy!" he said to me under his breath.

"What happened?"

"I was looking at that picture of Jesus over there and His halo came toward me and into my heart. Jesus is in my heart!"

Tears of joy flooded my eyes.

A woman in the congregation who was very ill came forward after the service for prayer. Johnny ran down the aisle after her, and as she knelt, he put his hand gently on her head. The healing happened immediately, just like in the Bible. I was full of awe as I witnessed the miracle.

I'd never believed in faith healing. I thought the people who professed to have been healed at services like Kathryn Kuhlman's were just imagining it. I'd never believed in evangelists either. I thought Billy Graham's ministry was a racket, and Oral Roberts was a con man. I hadn't realized what healing power is possible through God. Now I know these dedicated, wonderful people have had the same born-again experience I had, with the same Jesus Christ. They all are striving for the same thing—spreading the Good News to lost souls.

A month later, my daughter Karen, who had been a skeptic, accepted Jesus as her Lord and Savior after a chapel service in which a Gideon brother from Youth Defenders of America explained salvation. Karen asked Jesus into her heart, and the miracle took place.

Mother already knew that God was real and was deeply concerned—perhaps embarrassed is a better word—about my being a Jesus fanatic. She'd been raised a Catholic but had never had an experience such as mine, and doubted it was necessary.

But one day she said, "Joe, I've got to tell you what happened. I prayed real hard two nights ago, and after I went to bed, the room lit up and Jesus came into my heart!" She was radiant. "I felt like—I felt like I was re-re-"

"Reborn, mom. You felt like you were reborn. That's it."

Mom looked sparkling, and years seemed to drop off her age. All her aches and pains disappeared. She started telling her sons and daughters, everyone, about her rebirth in Christ.

I, too, was inspired to witness to practically everyone I saw. I carried my Bible with me always and studied it every spare moment. I observed how pastors and evangelists worked, trying to learn how to lead people in a sinner's prayer and to know Jesus Christ as their Lord.

The day I gave up all connections with the rackets, I simply told the boys, "You can have it all!"

Vince couldn't believe it. After all, it had taken years to build up this thing. Nobody puts in all that planning and struggling and then just walks away! But I did, and it was an important lesson to the boys and to me. Nobody in this day and age turns his back on free money—unless something supernatural happens to them. And it sure was happening to me!

Pappy came by one day with The Kid. I told them again of my experience, how the Spirit of God had told me to tell my friends. Pappy, who had spent some time in prison, was a well-known, rough, tough guy from the old school.

"You, know, Joe," he told me, "I read the Bible when I was in solitary."

I almost fell out of my chair! I couldn't help but notice how happy he looked as he talked about The Book.

"I didn't understand a lot of it, though," Pappy admitted.

I told him he'd have to accept Jesus Christ into his heart, and then the Power of God would help him understand.

"Joey, you're gonna be a minister."

"How did you know, Pappy?"

"My friend Jim Vaus is a minister. He'll introduce you to Billy Graham."

The Kid, who'd always been close to Pappy and me, looked confused. "Billy Graham? And Joe Donato? They just don't mix." His mind boggled at the idea.

The Kid always took orders from Pappy, and I felt Pappy could explain to him what I'd planned for my life. He could also soften the blow to all the boys in the underworld when the word got around that I'd decided to become an evangelist. God would work everything out, I knew.

My calling was to tell everyone of Jesus Christ and of heaven and hell. Knowing I had to reach those enmeshed in crime, I started going to the Burbank jail on Sundays. It was there I ran into Max Franklin, the preacher who had tried to tell me about Jesus ten years earlier. He remembered my name and was elated as we discussed my new life. He'd been praying for God to send him helpers in his ministry, and he accepted me as God's answer to his prayer.

My first visit to the Burbank jail had great significance for me. The massive steel doors looked very familiar. For the first time, I entered with a Bible in my hand instead of handcuffs on my wrists, and a minister with me instead of a police escort.

I glanced to my right. There was the cell that had held me when I was arrested in my first murder trial. It was empty, and I was glad . . . Now the walk down the corridor.

Max and I stared at the groups of men behind the bars.

"Howdy, fellas! We want to tell you about a plan for your life: how God so loved you He had His only begotten Son, Jesus, die for your sins."

Some listened. And some just lay on their bunks.

"I brought a man with me today who was with the underworld," Max said. "He'd like to tell you about his life."

All at once, it became very quiet. I felt the presence of the Holy Spirit as I passed them my police record and copies of rap sheets with mug shots taken when I was arrested. They couldn't help but see the great change in my face.

"I sat right where you are now, fellas—looking for the same answers you guys are searching for." I told them my life story, from the beginning.

At the end, I said, "You can sit with the devil and go to hell or stand up and come forward like a man to accept Jesus Christ as your personal Savior."

Every last one came forward, and we prayed together: "Oh, heavenly Father, be merciful to a sinner like me. I give Jesus my sins and accept Him in my heart as Lord and Savior. I know You accept me, God. Amen."

They all prayed aloud with their eyes closed and heads bowed. After the "Amen," I saw tears of joy streaming from some of their eyes. Jesus had forgiven their sins, and the miracle of God's hand had already touched them.

"I *feel* Him—I *feel* Him!" one Catholic boy exclaimed. "I never knew Jesus was alive. I feel heavenly and all clean inside me."

I counseled with the men and gave Bibles to everybody who wanted one. And then Max and I went to the next tank.

What a rewarding day that was! And it was just the beginning.

12

Driving home from that prison was heavenly. No looking in the rear-view mirror to see if a plainclothes detective was following me, no fear, no anxiety. Wonderful!

As I walked from my car to the house, I noticed a few of the neighbors gathered together talking.

"Hi, Joe, what's that book you're carrying?"

"It's my Bible! It's got all the answers for the whole world," I told them proudly. "I just came from the jail where I was preaching. I'm going to be an evangelist!" I could feel the Spirit of God within me as I told them this wonderful news.

The neighbors looked puzzled. They'd seen me in and out of so many scrapes with the law. They knew how I had treated my children and wife. They all loved Jean and felt a great pity for her, knowing what she'd been through on my account.

That settled it. Jean had to know about her new husband. Oh, she'd love this new guy! I went inside and put in a call to my mother-in-law in Salt Lake City.

"Ruth?" My mother-in-law had answered. "I must get ahold of Jean!" I was greatly excited.

"Joe? Jean isn't living here now. I don't know where she is."

"Ruth, let me tell you what happened to me. God came into my bedroom, and Jesus touched me. I'm reborn! I quit the rackets. I'm going to be a preacher. I love God! Oh, Ruth, it's beautiful! . . . Hello? Hello? Ruth, are you there?"

"Joe, are you all right?"

I'd forgotten for a moment about the old Joe, the only one she knew. I had to tell her about this miracle with Jesus, and I had to persuade her that I was telling the truth. It had all really happened. She seemed to be in a state of shock. Why should she believe me? I'd lied before and broken so many promises—

Her final words were, "Well, I'll tell Jean—but I find it all hard to believe."

In the next few weeks, I tried several times to trace Jean but with no success. Then one night, she called. I was so excited and happy, I just poured it all out. "Jean, honey, I love you! I need you. Did your mother tell you that Jesus came to me in my room? I'm reborn! I'm brand-new. Oh, what a life we're going to have! Jean, you must be reborn, too, so you won't go to hell. You'll know it when you experience the Spirit of God. Heaven comes into your heart! Honey, no more rackets or cursing or any of that old life. I'm going to be an evangelist. Oh, Jean, there's so much I want to tell you! When are you coming home?"

I think I said it all in one breath, and Jean thought I'd completely lost my mind. She was cold and adamant. I broke down and cried for real, something I'd never done before.

"Joe, I don't know what's going on, but you should know I've found a new life with somebody else. I don't love you anymore."

What a blow! It hurt from the top of my head to the bottom of my soul. I loved her so much.

"How are the kids, Joe?"

"Fine, fine! But we miss you very much, Jean."

"You hit me and threw me out, Joe. You put me through hell for too many years. I'm happy now. Don't cause me any trouble. Just leave me alone. I love those kids, but you killed all the love I ever had for you."

After she hung up, Joe, who always had all the answers, broke down and cried before the Lord. "Please help me, God!" I prayed and prayed and wept like a baby. I could feel His presence, and I was given strength and love to go on. I knew God would never fail me.

I was busy the next few weeks attending Bible classes, trying to digest every beautiful word in the Bible. And I continued asking for His help about Jean. Then one day, I was given an idea. Perhaps, if I could prove to Jean I wasn't lying about my changed life, if I could prove I was one who could be trusted—perhaps she'd return.

I drew up a petition stating "I, Joe Donato, take all blame and responsibility for all the things that happened to Jean. It was all my fault; I was wrong." There were some other facts in the paper, too; I'd given it some serious thought. I took the petition around for signatures—to Jean's friends, the neighbors, the PTA, my brothers, and our kids. Even my old pal Vince signed it. Most everyone I approached was glad to add his name. Some of them sobbed.

In real humility, I mailed it to Jean in care of her mother's address. I knew this would do it! Anxiously, I waited for a fruitful reply. Surely she'd call, and we'd all be reunited.

Instead, when Jean called, it was a rerun of our last conversation. She was happy in her new life; it was over between us; I was supposed to forget her.

I really couldn't blame her. How could a lunatic like

115

Joe change so completely? If the shoe had been on the other foot, I'd have thought she was crazy. I knew that if she could only have the rebirth experience I'd had, she'd know it was possible to have a truly new life and be a new person. All I could do was pray that it would happen to Jean, and that someday soon we'd all be together again. I'd never quit trying to get her back.

Some weeks later, I had a phone call from a government man who asked me to meet him for breakfast in a restaurant in the San Fernando Valley. He had heard about my changed life and wanted to know more about it.

As we sat talking, I was reminded that he and other FBI men had been trying for fifteen years to put me in prison. And now I was telling him about how God had transformed me from a criminal to a believer ministering for Jesus Christ. At first, he was skeptical. He had arranged our meeting to find out what new angle I'd come up with. Surely Joe Donato was on this religious kick to make money!

The FBI man finally admitted that he, too, was a Christian and could tell I was sincere, that I truly had been born again.

"Wait till I tell the fellows in the police department! They heard the rumor, but they figured you'd gone out of your mind."

I met him again for breakfast a week or so later. Then he got straight to the point.

"We have an assignment worked out for you if you'll take it."

"An assignment?" I was puzzled. "I don't get you, Jack."

"Well, Joe, you know the underworld. We want you to go back and be an informer for us."

"You must be kidding! Most of the boys think I'm nuts because I go chasing them with a Bible in my hand instead of a gun in my pocket. Can you imagine me going back into the rackets?" The idea was preposterous! I was sure he'd realize this.

I went on, "I couldn't even act the part. When Jesus came to me, He told me to tell my friends. That's what I'm going to do: tell them about Jesus Christ."

Our talk then turned to prison reform. I told them that prisons were needed, but our system was not working, that most of the men, women, boys, and girls who came out of penal institutions were worse than when they went in.

"They are training areas for the devil!"

He agreed. "Then what is the answer to the soaring crime rate? We're being submerged in it."

"There's only one answer, Jack."

"And that is?"

"Jesus Christ. If He could change a lunatic like me into a human being concerned with saving souls for Him, He can do it to others. I'm going to dedicate my life to going into prisons, and speaking to men and women about my experience. I'm going to try to keep them from going into the hell I put myself through with the devil!"

"That's a pretty big assignment."

"I know. But God can change anybody. All they have to do is want to be changed. Everyone is worth saving."

When we parted, we were the best of friends, and agreed on all these points. But he was convinced I would never inform on the underworld for the FBI or for anyone else.

His parting shot was, "So you're going to be a Holy Joe! Who would ever have believed this?" He shook his head and walked toward his car.

I immediately went to see some of my former associates and told them about my meeting with the FBI man. I wanted them to know that I'd been asked to become an informer and had refused. I found out later that an underworld character had been in that restaurant and had seen me talking to the government man. When he

117

reported it to the boys and nervously said it didn't look good to him, they were able to assure him he needn't worry—Joe had already told them all about it.

One day, I decided to visit KHOF, the radio and television station I'd been listening to constantly since God's hand had turned my radio to it. I drove to Glendale where their facilities are located, met everyone there, and told them something about my life. They were amazed—stunned—and introduced me to Pastor Schoch who invited me to attend his services at Faith Center.

Faith Center was a bright, happy place with rousing music, stirring sermons, and enthusiastic, born-again Christians. I couldn't help but liken it in a way to what we called "The Happy Church" in our neighborhood in Reading. It was a Negro church—a poor, ramshackle building—and on meeting nights it was the loudest place on the block. I didn't understand then how people could get so happy and wrought-up over religion. Such swinging singing—such loud praising of the Lord! We thought they were nuts. But after Jesus came into my heart, I could identify with this kind of holy commotion.

After a few weeks, Pastor Schoch invited me to give my testimony on television and radio. I was so happy. If just one soul were saved or one life changed, it would be worth everything to me. I agreed to appear, and the date was set. I also began attending their Bible study classes every week and enjoyed learning all about God's Word.

In the meantime, John and Karen, my beautiful children, asked me to take them to the beach one afternoon. It sounded like a good idea. I had been so busy in His work that I'd not taken any time for any relaxation. While my children were romping in the waves, I walked on the sand and enjoyed the clean, warm air. When I noticed a large group of teenagers sitting nearby, I strolled over and stood in the middle of their circle, with a Bible in my hand.

"Guys and girls, I'm going to tell you the story of

118

my life."

As they sat there, skeptical at first but listening politely, their eyes widened with interest and wonder. I told them all about my life with the devil; then I related the beautiful story of God's love through Jesus Christ and told them how He had spoken to me and come into my heart.

They were amazed, and started to ask all kinds of questions. Before long, some of them accepted Christ as their Savior. One boy in particular, who looked like a typical hippie, was really touched by the hand of God, and the tears flowed down his face.

"Say, Joe, what does Jesus really look like?"

"I don't know," I replied. "I really don't know." When I'd met Jesus in my bedroom that morning, I had seen nothing, just felt His Presence and heard His message.

I chatted with them for a long time, gave them some Christian literature, and advised them to find a good Gospel-preaching church to attend. Now that they'd been born again, they would want to learn all they could about their Savior.

That night, I asked my Heavenly Father to let me see His Son. I wanted to tell everybody in prisons, youth rallies, churches, on television—wherever He'd send me—what our Savior looks like.

I really didn't think that God would honor my prayer, but several weeks later, at two o'clock on a Sunday morning (the time of the appearance of that light I'd seen when John was ill), I was awakened suddenly. As I looked up, I saw Him! He was about four feet away from me, gazing toward the East. The vision was heavenly, but I was terrified! My heart felt as if it would jump out of my chest. My eyes closed in fear. Then the picture came back into my mind. I opened my eyes. His face had moved right up in front of me.

He had olive skin and dark hair. His beard was well-trimmed and came up rather close to His eyes. His thick

119

hair was not long—only down past the base of His neck. His nose was straight and aquiline. His dark eyes seemed sad, but they reflected great love, and they could see to the depths of my soul.

He was a simple, plain person who would go unnoticed in a crowd. It pleased me that there was no look of femininity about Him as in so many artists' portrayals. In fact, He was decidedly masculine.

I lay in bed for two hours, shaking like a leaf, sweating profusely. Finally, I got on my knees and thanked Almighty God for this beautiful vision. My voice trembled as I prayed.

This happened on a Sunday morning—a very important Sunday for me, as it was the day I was to give my testimony at KHOF in Glendale.

I was nervous that night as I stepped in front of the microphone, but God soon calmed me down. I proceeded to tell the audience of around eight hundred in the church, plus a viewing audience of thousands, the story of my life. As I described my years of crime and told of being born again, the hall was so quiet you could have heard a pin drop. After I'd talked for twenty minutes, I left the stage and was immediately encircled by the wonderful brothers and sisters who rushed forward to shake my hand and embrace me with love and compassion. We all had the same Father. Tears of joy flooded my eyes.

As I drove home, I went over my speech in my mind. I knew many of the boys from the old life had known about my debut on television, and I had prayed they would watch it. In my testimony, I took the blame for all the crimes I had committed; I didn't incriminate any of the boys.

The next day, the phone began ringing like crazy!

"Hey, Joey! What a speech!" The Kid exclaimed. "What a speech! I can't get over it!"

"It's all true—every word of it," I told him.

A few days later, the wife of one of the guys called and

said that her spaghetti dinner had gotten cold while the boys were in the den watching me on television. She said they listened silently, and after the broadcast was over, she heard them cheering for me and the great job I'd done.

I had to laugh over a call I had from one of the boys.

"Joey, I just figured it out! You're going to print Bibles! What an idea! Let me in on it!"

"Bibles? Me? Print Bibles?" I answered with surprise. "I'm not printing them, but a lot of people give them away—including me."

He was obsessed with the idea, and within a week, the rumor had spread everywhere. Guys were phoning to ask when I was going to start printing my own Bible. I wondered if they thought I was going to write a "Joe's Version," but as far as I was concerned, the Bible was perfect just as it was. After all, it was God's Word.

My story had made a great impact on the television audience, and I was suddenly in demand as a speaker. I spoke in churches, prisons, reform schools, youth rallies, and Full Gospel Business Men's dinners. They were all rewarding experiences.

One question I heard often was, "Aren't you afraid of your old friends—of being killed?"

I thought for a moment before answering: "My life is in God's hands. Nothing is going to happen to me till He calls me home. And if I lose this life for His sake, Jesus promised I'd live forever. I know without a doubt this is true.

"My God opened the seas for the children of Israel and knocked down the walls of Jericho with a trumpet blast. He is the same today, and His hand is on me."

About this time, I dug into my cache of "dirty money" and started pouring it out into God's work. I'd made it while aligned with Satan, but now it belonged to God. I wanted Him to take everything I had and use it for His glory. None of the riches of this world could make me

turn from Jesus Christ or buy from me the real treasure
I had in my heart.

13

The Baptism in the Holy Spirit—I'd heard a great deal about it, and had asked a number of people to pray for me to receive it. I expected an explosion of lights and pinwheeling colors or something, but each time, I was disappointed.

Then one day, a kind, and very wise, Christian brother suggested to me that perhaps I had already received the infilling of the Holy Spirit, and all I needed was to let what was inside me flow forth.

That night, kneeling by the side of my bed, I asked God to help me manifest the gift that He had already given me. I praised Him, raising my hands in the air, and venturing a few random syllables. All of a sudden, I was praising Him in a new language! It was almost as if I was listening to another person pray. What's more, I knew the prayer was coming straight from the heart, spirit to Spirit, without being contaminated by my own thoughts or desires. I lost all track of time and space, and let His love enfold me. If only life could be like this forever!

But it wasn't long before I found that even the new life was not all a bowl of cherries.

One day my daughter Karen became quite upset because I had been the cause of her mother leaving.

"I hate you, daddy!" she screamed.

I tried to calm her down, to console her.

"Honey, I'm doing all I can to get mom to come back," I said, but she ran to her room and slammed the door. Tears began to well up in my eyes, and I got down on my knees.

"God, help me!" I prayed. "Give me strength. My daughter is so lonely. I get lonely, too, Lord. Please help us both."

I sobbed uncontrollably for ten minutes. Then, suddenly, all the pressures were released. I felt God's loving hand reach out to me, imparting His peace that passes all understanding.

Karen came back into the living room while I was still on my knees. "I'm sorry, daddy," she said gently. "It's just that I get so lonesome for mom. I miss her so much." Her eyes and the tone of her voice told me God had touched her, too, and she had forgiven me. I had to remind her—and myself—that no one is ever *really* lonely if he walks with Jesus.

Ever since my conversion, I had been disturbed over my status with the Internal Revenue Service. One day, I called Jack, my FBI friend, and told him I felt I ought to pay income tax on $40,000 of unreported income for the last two years. He made an appointment for me at the IRS. As I drove to keep the appointment, I felt very happy—and so clean inside. After all, how could I preach with honesty unless I had my affairs straightened out?

As I entered the IRS office, I prayed, "God, You led me here. I'm in Your hands."

Two men greeted me and introduced themselves. I

could read their minds. They were thinking, "What's Joe Donato up to? He's full of angles."

A mild-mannered agent asked, "What made you come here?"

I told them of my life in crime, and my various convictions, of which they were already aware. Then I described my rebirth experience—how God through His Son Jesus had spoken to me in my bedroom and saved my soul. Next, I proceeded to give them a sermon on the importance of accepting Christ as one's Savior. The two men listened quietly for over fifteen minutes.

It was several months later when I returned to the office. A new man had been assigned to my case— a soft-spoken young agent. After we were introduced, I began talking to him about God's plan of salvation.

"Richard, I feel God has His hand on you."

"I'm Catholic, Joe. I guess I'm a Christian."

"Friend, if you guess, then you're not. I've known many Catholics who thought they were right with God, but when they really asked Him to come into their hearts and take away their sins, they had wonderful experiences of rebirth. Richard, you have to be born again and walk in God's way."

He listened with interest for a long while as I told him how Jesus had said, "Unless a man be born again, he cannot see the Kingdom of God."

Finally, we spent fifteen minutes talking about my income tax.

A month later, when I was at KHOF in Glendale taping a show, Richard showed up with a beautiful girl, an IRS agent who was a radiant born-again Christian. After I was free, she and I sat with Richard between us and talked about God's plan for him for nearly an hour. Eventually, we got down to the facts on my tax case. A few weeks later, the young agent called to tell me he had started reading the Bible and was very close to accepting Christ as his personal Savior.

Then began my twice-weekly TV appearances, during which I interviewed people who testified that they had tried everything, then finally accepted Jesus Christ and found that He was the answer, no matter what the problem. I hosted ex-drug addicts, ex-murderers, ex-criminals—lost sinners until Christ changed their lives. I also interviewed chaplains and policemen who had unusual stories about the mercy of God.

About this time, my mother decided to return to Pennsylvania. She had helped me tremendously, and I was grateful. I thanked God she'd come to help when I was so desperate, but most of all, I thanked Him that she was walking more closely with God. I knew He'd give me the strength and wisdom I needed to take over the household work and the raising of my kids.

I had to plan my time carefully. As I became more involved in God's work, my days were crowded. I had to keep the house in shape, do the shopping and cooking, take the kids to school, and still manage to tape my programs, study the Bible, attend classes and services, talk to groups, and help in rehabilitation homes.

I met a lot of interesting people as I traveled in the new circles God had opened to me. Phil Thatcher was one dynamic Christian I was especially happy to meet, because his background was quite similar to mine. Phil had spent thirteen years in prisons and reform schools, and then was reborn. Subsequently, he dedicated his life to saving souls. He goes into prisons and reform schools, preaching the good news of Jesus Christ.

Phil's wife, Marie, works along with him, and together they've opened up many boys' camps for the underprivileged. Phil had a plan to help ex-convicts obtain jobs after their release and later was hired by Job Therapy of California. He finds pen pals (no pun intended) who write to men in prisons and even visit them when the jails are nearby.

Phil's organization also rounds up jobs and accommodations for men and women who have served their sentences. I have been able to be a part of this program, too, with TV requests for people to help in rehabilitating ex-convicts. Many prisoners cannot be released because they have no jobs and nowhere to go.

Phil and I also visit Christian homes, such as those being run by Teen Challenge, where ex-drug addicts live in a wholesome environment while readjusting their lives. Teen Challenge has proven over and over that even hard-core addicts can be cured immediately with no withdrawal agonies when the addict accepts Christ and asks for His forgiveness and help.

One of the men Phil helped was Jim Tucker—a six-foot-four two-hundred-and-forty-five pounder. He had spent twenty-seven years in reform schools and prisons since he was nine. Jim was a drug user, burglar, robber—you name it! He'd done everything except murder and had been on the FBI's most-wanted list. Because he was crazy as well as incorrigible, they placed him in a cell with no clothing except his shorts for three years. Jim's food was placed on paper plates and shoved under the door, because no guard wanted to risk being beaten with his huge fists. His dream was to get out of prison, mount a machine gun on a jeep, and kill as many policemen as he could in front of City Hall.

After many years, it was time for Jim to come up for parole. He wrote a hundred and fifty letters asking people for help and received not one answer. Then someone suggested he write Phil Thatcher. He did, though by then he was so skeptical he bet another inmate twenty-five dollars that Phil wouldn't reply. He lost the bet. Within a week, Phil had answered Jim's letter and had gone to see him. Jim lost no time in letting Phil know that he didn't like Christians—especially preachers.

"You're the kind of hardheaded sucker I like to help!" was Phil's joyful reaction. It wasn't long until he'd used his influence to have Jim released to his custody.

It was a new experience for Jim with these sincere, loving Christians. He was deeply touched when they celebrated his first birthday as a free man and gave him the first birthday cake he'd ever had in his whole life.

Several months later, Jim found himself on his bedroom floor praying to God, and Jesus came into his heart. His life was completely changed, and he has joined Phil and me often in witnessing in churches and prisons and at businessmen's dinners. He is especially forceful in his message to prisoners, telling how he found the answer after so many useless, searching years. Youngsters are greatly impressed with his story, and he has set many on the right road to salvation.

After I had been on television for a while, I was invited to go to Hartford, Connecticut, to appear on Channel 18, a station recently acquired by Faith Center in Glendale. Although I dreaded flying, I was eager to bring my story to a wider audience. Two of my neighbors were kind enough to keep the children while I was gone, so I had no worries about them. Gary Baker, an executive of KHOF and a brother Christian, accompanied me on the flight. As soon as we got on the plane, God removed all fear, and I was soon talking about my favorite subject, Jesus Christ, to the stewardess and one of the passengers.

We were met at the airport by Bill Finley, the man who ran Channel 18 in Hartford. For the next week, I was busy giving my story on his station, visiting churches, and talking to youth groups. I loved every moment of it and thanked God for the opportunity to witness for Christ. I prayed that I'd be instrumental in preventing many people from taking the road I had traveled for so many years. Everywhere I went, I also prayed for the sick, and God answered many of those prayers.

One night, I gave a two-hour testimony on television. The program went on right after a popular hockey game, during which they showed my police mug shots instead of commercials. We had a large viewing audience, with ten people answering phones. The response was wonderfully heartwarming, and all of God. No amount of money could have bought my happiness. This show was taped and sent to stations in other states.

Since it was only two hours to Pennsylvania by plane, I went to visit my relatives. It was good to see them again. They had heard of my new life, and before I left, nine of them accepted Christ after listening to my story.

It had occurred to me that I should have a station wagon for my work in California. I needed the space to carry the many Bibles, books, and tracts I give away in my ministry. My car was just too small. Although many of the boys in the underworld owed me money from loans, no one was about to pay "Holy Joe" these days! I couldn't blame them. After all, instead of shooting them full of holes, I was trying to fill them with the Word of God and salvation. I didn't want one soul going to hell if I could help it.

One day in Reading, I ran into Sammy, a man who knew all the ins and outs of the underworld. I reminded him he owed me money.

"Sam, I could use that money you owe me in my ministry."

He knew of what had happened in my life and was happy for me, but he said, "Joe, I'm a little short of cash because of the floods." I knew the recent floods had devastated some property in which he had an interest.

I thought, Oh well, Joe, you really didn't expect him to pay you anyway, did you?

Then Sam said, "Hey, wait a minute, Joe! I've got a new station wagon you could have shipped to California."

God was giving me the desires of my heart.

There was one prison I had to visit in Reading, but I needed an entree. I went to the Detective Bureau in City Hall.

129

"Where can I find John Habecker?" I inquired of the girl at the desk.

On the intercom, she reached John and told him a Joe Donato wanted to see him. Immediately he came out of his office with his hand extended.

"John, first I want to apologize for all the past," I told him as we went into his office. On the desk was a beautiful, old, well-worn Bible. It gave me the opening to tell him about the miraculous experience I had had in my bedroom when I had been reborn.

The lieutenant talked to me about his Christian life and what it had meant to him, and we reminisced about old times. I told him I wanted to go into Berks County Prison where I'd been sent twenty-four years previously for pointing a gun at him. He gave me some advice on how to approach it. And after getting in touch with the warden, I was scheduled to appear that Sunday for a prison service.

It was snowing and bitter cold as I went through the first door. Then the second steel door clanged shut, and I smiled to myself, knowing I could walk out that same day.

We opened the service with some beautiful hymns while the prisoners filed into the chapel. I told them of my life of crime, my conversion and dedication to God's work as an evangelist. The room became very quiet.

"Men, you have been judged so many times," I told them. "Now you be the judge and the jury. I'll give you some Bible facts as well as scientific facts. This is going to be the most important discussion of your lives. Bring in your own verdict.

"Almost two thousand years ago, the disciples of Jesus asked, 'When will the end come?' Jesus turned to them and said these prophetic words: 'For many shall come in my name saying I am the Christ and shall deceive many.' Then He told them, 'Ye shall hear of wars and rumors of wars. See that ye be not troubled, for all these things must come to pass. But the end is not yet. For nation shall rise against nation and kingdom against kingdom; and there shall be famines and pestilences and earthquakes in diverse places. And this gospel of the Kingdom shall be preached in all the world for a witness unto all nations. And then shall the end come.' This was written in the Bible in the twenty-fourth chapter of Matthew."

They were all listening, and a few were nodding in agreement. I said a silent, fast prayer of thanks, and then went on "Now, fellas, here are the scientific facts: six hundred million men, women, and children have died in wars. And it's proven nothing. 'But Joe,' you say, 'we always have wars.' Yes. But at one time, one spear could kill only one person at a time. Then the cannonball was invented, and it might destroy seven. A German shell in World War I killed eighty-seven; then by the second World War, we had atomic bombs capable of annihilating one hundred thousand people. Today, in a nuclear war, a hundred million could be killed in the first hour before the other nation could even get started with its own nuclear weapons. Do you realize that today there is stockpiled the equivalent of over a quarter of a ton of TNT for every man, woman, and child on the earth?"

Most prisoners have seen too much to shock easily, but still a low murmur went through the room. I continued. "The Bible says a great holocaust will come on the earth in which one-third of the world will be destroyed: plants, animal life, people—everything! There will be a fire from the heavens, and a great earthquake. Did you know that the earth is ninety-nine percent fire? We live on an eight-mile crust. Inside is great heat. Every quake opens the many faults in our planet more and more. Two hundred years ago, there were two thousand quakes a year. Now there's one every minute.

"Since World War II, we have had kingdoms fighting within kingdoms: Korea, Africa, Bangladesh, Vietnam,

131

Ireland. Sixty-five million people have been killed in China. Millions have been killed in the Communist quest for world domination. The United States, once the leading power, is more and more divided on issues. Our resources are dwindling, and crime, racial hatred, moral decay, and many other things have weakened the country tremendously.

"The Bible tells about famine in the last days. It's a fact that last year twenty-five million people starved to death. It's hard for us to believe, for we grow sixty percent of the world's food, yet have only six percent of the world's population. One hundred and thirty-two people are being born every minute. How can we feed these millions?

"We read about pestilences, and we know the word is allied with the word 'pollution.' Everyone is becoming aware that forty percent of the plankton in the ocean is dead and the fish will not survive long. Our waters are polluted, and so is the air we breathe."

Now every one of them was concentrating on what I was saying. It was time to tie it all together. "The Holy Scriptures are being fulfilled, yet people refuse to accept the facts. For those of us who know the Lord, this is a thrilling time, for we know our Lord will soon return. But many will die horrible deaths before then. I ask you —what kind of God would leave you here to perish when the end comes? I wouldn't worship that God! But He gave us a way out. We were separated from Him because of our sinful natures. Then He had His Son, Jesus Christ, die on a cross for our sins. If you accept Christ, He will lead you to heaven and eternal life. Yes, the price has been paid. God made it that easy. That's why a lot of people will go to hell. Because salvation is too easy.

"God said that a thousand years is like a day. If you live to an old age, you're here for just a few hours. But— where are you going to spend eternity? Eternal hell or eternal heaven? The Bible says that in hell, there is a weeping and gnashing of teeth forever."

I paused and took the time to look at each one of them. "Everyone here must stand before God for judgment. If you accept Jesus Christ, He will plead your case—and He's never lost one yet! He's a physician, lawyer, and comforter. If any of you are candidates for a miracle in your lives, come forward. You're not doing it to honor Joe Donato. You're walking down here to meet Jesus Christ as your personal Savior. . .

"What's the verdict, jury?"

It had been a long sermon, but the men sat still hanging on every word. I quoted some of my favorite passages from the Bible: "For whosoever shall call upon the name of the Lord shall be saved." "Jesus said, 'If you confess me before men, I'll confess you before my Father and the angels in heaven. But if you deny me before men, I'll deny you before my Father and the angels in heaven.' What is your decision, men?"

The Holy Spirit reached out into the service, and many prisoners came forward. But something wasn't right—on one side were black men and on the other, a mass of white men.

"Fellas," I said, "you're soon going to be brothers in Christ. So join hands in Christian love!" The inmates formed a large circle, joining hands. Two guards moved forward quickly. For a moment, I wondered if I'd gone too far with the holding-hands bit! But then the guards approached the middle of the chain and grasped the prisoners' hands to make an even larger circle! I started to pray, and soon we were all praying out loud.

"Heavenly Father, we thank Jesus for dying for our sins. We give You all our sins—You know what they are. We accept Jesus in our hearts as Lord and Savior of our lives. We know, Jesus, You've accepted us. We know You are alive today. So touch our lives and hearts. Thank You, God, for Your gift of eternal life! Amen."

I left Pennsylvania in a few days, thanking God for such a fruitful trip.

133

It was great to be back with my kids, but I knew we'd never be completely happy without their mom. I was still trying to get her to come back, but the scars of hurt were too deeply imbedded in her heart. I vowed I'd keep on trying till my dying day. The kids missed her so much, and I wanted a chance to make up to her for all the hurt and anguish I'd caused her.

I was soon back into my busy routine. Now and then, I saw my old underworld pals, and they watched me often on television. I learned what faithful listeners they were one night when my program was pre-empted. The phone started to ring soon after the scheduled time.

"Hey, Joe! You're not on tonight!" It was Vince.

One night, he invited me to his place for dinner. Another guest was an attractive friend of Vince's girl. She had watched my program and was eager to meet me. Before I left that night, she had accepted Christ as her Savior and Lord.

Vince phones me often and at times comes to talk—but mainly to listen intently as I tell him about God's Word and His plan for our lives. Sometimes he stays very late, and I feel that his conversion is not far away. I pray that it happens soon. Then he can be a witness to the old gang, too!

14

Not long after my Eastern trip, I received an invitation to go to Seattle, Washington, with Nick Cadena—an ex-addict who runs three homes to help people get off drugs and find a new life in Christ—and Louie, a Mexican ex-addict and former convict. We were to speak in a Roman Catholic Church, then visit the federal prison on McNeil Island. I agreed to go, for the trip offered wonderful opportunities for witnessing. My neighbors—bless their hearts—offered to take care of my boy and girl once more.

We were met at the Seattle airport by some wonderful Christian brothers. One of the men who greeted us was a born-again Catholic priest. His congregation of two thousand people had all accepted Christ and lived close to Him. The priest practiced the Word of God instead of just going through the motions. He was praying that the Pope would give out the message that a person must accept Jesus personally to gain eternal life.

As we waited at the boat landing to go to McNeil Island, the air was clean and fresh, the wind bitter cold and hard. We boarded the ferry at 7:30 in the morning, along with twenty-five or thirty guards for the next shift at the prison. Louie knew many of them, as he had spent several years confined on McNeil. Almost before we were on board, he began telling them about his new life, and apologized to each one for the thoughts he had had of them in the past.

When our boat arrived at the dock, Chaplain Siders was there to meet us. After a long walk across the dock, we faced the front gate of the prison. The island seemed to be very beautiful, but the prison itself was grim-looking. At a signal, someone at the tower opened the main gate and we went in. After going through the second gate, Louie spotted some old buddies.

"Hey, Louie!" they yelled. "What are you doing here? You look great, Lou!"

Tears filled Louie's eyes as he answered them in Spanish. He was so happy to be back, bringing them God's message, but was sad to see his old lost friends still behind prison walls.

We were taken at once to the chapel, past the lines of prisoners who were going to the services. Louie stopped to talk to some of them, and several of them began to weep as they heard the story of his new life. They remarked over and over again how good he looked, how changed he was!

After the men had filed into the attractive chapel, the chaplain said a few words, then a choir of men convicts sang. They were superb. I knew from their joy and sincerity that they were brothers in Christ.

Nick introduced Louie, who gave an anointed testimony with love, understanding, and concern. The crowd was silent and attentive.

Next, I told the story of my life in crime and all the bitterness, hate, and greed I had experienced.

Nick also spoke, giving his testimony and concluding with his favorite quotation from the Bible: "For God so loved the world that he gave his only begotten Son, that whosoever believeth in him should not perish, but have everlasting life." Then he challenged the men with, "If you're a candidate for everlasting life, come forward and meet Jesus!"

The altar call was overwhelming. Among those who pressed forward to accept Christ were some in their early twenties as well as a few as old as seventy. They confessed their sins, asked to be forgiven, and invited Jesus to come into their hearts. Some of them wept with joy as they were reborn. Afterward, we talked to them for a long time, and before we left, we exchanged names and addresses so we could correspond.

That night, we gave our testimonies at the large Catholic church headed by our Spirit-filled priest. After we had talked, a healing service was held. One man with an Eastern European accent said, "I can't get heat into my body. I was in a Communist prison in Europe for years, and now I can't get warm—but I know the power of God is going to heal me tonight!"

The whole church seemed to be full of the Holy Spirit! It was like electricity all around—accelerating my pulse, thrilling my heart. Into my mind came the memory of God's words to me, *Touch and heal.* I touched my hands lightly on the man's forehead and prayed for his healing. Suddenly, I felt a great heat flowing through my hands and into his body.

The man started to perspire freely, and in joy he cried out, "I'm healed! I'm healed!"

He seemed to be aglow with light as he tugged at my suit jacket and said, "Please pray for my wife. She can hardly walk!"

I found his wife, a simple peasant-like person who was about eight-months pregnant.

"Do you think Jesus can heal you?" I asked her.

"Oh yes, I know He can!"

As I placed my hands on her head, I prayed, "Dear God, in the name of Jesus, heal this body!" Then that same heat penetrated my hands and her body, and I knew God had healed her.

She stood up, crying with joy, and walked—without pain.

The third person to ask for healing was a beautiful young woman who had a severe ear infection. My hand was on her ear as I prayed, and we both felt the same heat as she was instantly healed.

It was the Spirit of God—using me. I did not have anything to do with the healing. Only God can perform miracles. But he gave me a tremendous gift of faith. That night, I *knew* that the Lord would use me as a channel for His healing for each person who asked for prayer.

After the service, the priest invited us to a late dinner where we sang and prayed as we enjoyed turkey and all the trimmings. It had been a wonderfully thrilling and rewarding day.

I had dug into what money I had left to pay our expenses. I had learned that if you are a Christian and want to see God in action, you must give Him your all— body, heart, soul, talents, and money. What you put into His work will build up your heavenly savings account for eternity. And He will pay interest tenfold on all you've given Him.

When I returned home and opened the mail, I found a large check, an unexpected gift which helped pay for much of our trip. I was learning more and more about how He provides for us when we trust Him.

15

One of the brightest moments of my first year as a Christian was Christmas. Now that I knew the true meaning of Christmas, everything took on a new luster. I remembered the old Yuletide holidays—buying gifts, trying to outdo everyone else, eating, drinking, following the leaders and going through the hollow motions of enjoyment. But in 1972, for the first time, Christmas to me was the birthday of Jesus, the Son of God, who had delivered my life from eternal hell. Now I was His, spreading His Good News and His plan for eternal life.

I remembered all the men, women, and children who'd repeated the sinner's prayer with me and accepted Christ, the miracles I had witnessed, the lost souls I'd counseled. It had been a wonderful year. All that was lacking as the new year began was Jean. The children and I missed her so much. I was still praying for a chance to make up for all the scars I'd inflicted on her heart.

The new year brought a heavy schedule of speaking engagements. Every one was a spiritual thrill for me. Often I would be given the offerings collected at these meetings. I was a bit embarrassed about this, though I matched these amounts ten to one from my racket money. I had many expenses connected with my evangelism—mainly travel costs and the purchase of literature to give away. I never went to a prison or a Christian Home empty-handed.

The joy I felt at this new endeavor was indescribable. God's love and concern gave me back far more than I ever put into His work. Just seeing hopeless addicts completely cured with no withdrawal pains when they accepted Jesus was reward enough.

And then one day, a message from Jean raised my hopes and those of the children—she was coming to visit! At last I'd have a chance to show Jean a new life full of meaning and love. I'd introduce her to all my new friends who had joined me in prayers for her and our marriage. There was no way in the world that she wouldn't be able to see the great change in me. Surely, God would touch her life, too!

Bubbling over with excitement, like a kid with his first birthday party, I cleaned the house from top to bottom, spruced up the yard, and got everything in tip-top shape. The kids were elated to help prepare for the visit of their mother whom they had missed so very much. Oh, how I thanked God for giving me a new chance to make amends to my wife!

We all sang as we drove to the airport to meet Jean. While we waited for the plane, I kept thinking, "What will I say to her? How will I begin? Will she see the big change in me? Will she forgive me?" I prayed that God would give me wisdom and guidance.

Finally, the big jet arrived and the passengers filed out. My heart was beating hard with anticipation.

The kids spotted Jean first and made a dash for her.

Kisses were mingled with tears of joy as John and Karen greeted their mom. I held back for a moment, eager to begin apologizing for the hurt I'd caused her, wanting to tell her all the things I was going to do to make amends. "Oh, Lord," I prayed. "This is beautiful—wonderful!"

I finally got my chance, and I squeezed in to hug and kiss her after so many months of loving and wanting. The tears brimmed in my eyes as I put my arms around her, but Jean turned her face away abruptly, and my kiss glanced off her cheek. A bullet or knife could not have caused more pain.

Embarrassed, I said, "Honey, you sure look good!" Then I stammered, "Jean, I'm so sorry for all the things I've done to you!" Her eyes were cold, her lips unsmiling. "Jean, please forgive me. I love you. I really do."

The kids took it all in, still happy and excited. They were probably remembering the days when their old dad cursed and beat their mom. That Joe had been an animal—the lowest of the low! Now they had a father who was full of love and understanding.

Jean cut in with, "Joe, please! I'm tired." We started moving toward the escalator. "Of course she's tired," I thought. "Maybe later we can talk things over, and she'll be more receptive."

Through it all, I felt a Hand upon my shoulder, giving me strength and calmness.

As soon as we arrived at the house, my wife disappeared to visit the neighbors. They had all been very fond of her, and having Jean back was exciting for them, too.

That first day, the kids couldn't get enough of their mom. There was so much to catch up with! That night, when Jean and I tucked the children into their beds, their eyes sparkled with happiness.

As we left their rooms, I slipped my arm around Jean's shoulders. Again she pulled away with an indifferent motion, and I realized I'd been kidding myself.

141

"Joe," she explained, "I have a new life with someone else. Can't you understand? I don't love you anymore."

How those words cut! My hopes seemed to be lost.

She continued, "Don't try to put your arms around me or kiss me. I don't want to hurt your feelings, but you'll have to leave me alone. Don't make me feel bad. I'm here because of the kids."

That night, I lay in bed thinking and praying. There was my wife asleep in the next room. Only a wall separated us, yet it seemed like a million miles.

For the next ten days, I tried in every way to show kindness, but Jean remained aloof. I couldn't blame her, and I tried very hard to show her that I was a new Joe. However, when love is gone, it's gone. Jean talked about getting a divorce, splitting up what we had, and having custody of the children. I tried to get out of talking these things over with her, but she had made up her mind.

I finally agreed to everything except giving up the children. I wanted them raised in a Christian, God-centered home. Some of our most precious moments were when I'd read the Bible to them and teach them about Jesus.

"What do you kids want to do?" I asked them. After all, they weren't babies. Karen was a young lady, nearly fourteen.

"We'd like to go with mom."

"Are you sure that's what you really want?"

"Dad," Karen said, taking my arm, "you are so involved in your work—going to prisons, preaching, and everything. You come home late at night, and we have to stay at the neighbors' houses *so* often. You don't spend much time with us anymore. If mom lived close, we could be with her and still see you."

I didn't argue with them. It was a matter for God to take care of. I *was* spending less time with them, but I was deeply involved in God's work, and that had to be a top priority.

After Jean returned to Utah, there were many phone calls concerning the divorce. Jean couldn't make up her mind whether she wanted to live in California or Utah.

In the meantime, my TV show, "Prisoners," was gaining momentum. The mail stayed heavy, and people were opening their hearts and pocketbooks in response to what I was trying to do. They always said they were praying for me, and I loved them all for it.

Every dollar that came in was used for producing the program and helping prisoners, and I matched every dollar contributed with four of my own. But my savings wouldn't last forever. Sometime in the near future, I was going to need an income. I knew my Father would provide it. I once had made thousands of dollars a week but had no peace. Now I had thousands going out, directed to God's glory and work, and felt a beautiful joy. Nothing was more rewarding than helping others to know the Christ I'd met.

My church speaking engagements were building up as well as engagements for other Christian groups. For a while, I actually had to turn down some of them. I didn't want to neglect the prisons. They always came first.

One day I was invited to tell my story at Youth Defenders in Sylmar, California, an organization striving to help young men and women whose lives had seemed hopeless. The founder was Irene Sullivan, a wonderful Christian woman who had been stricken with cancer five years before. Doctors told her that her days were numbered, but God had different plans, and He healed her completely.

The needs at this Home were tremendous, I could see, and that night after I'd given my testimony, I made a donation toward her work.

As I drove home, I prayed that God would put more money in my hands so I could help others. I was moved to tears as I asked that I might supply the necessities of all these newborn people. "God, so much is needed! Help me, Jesus!"

143

I had a hiding place in my home where I had, in the old days, stashed some of my "weekly pay envelopes." Since my conversion, I'd been making steady inroads into this fund until the last envelope had been withdrawn.

However, for some unexplainable reason, as soon as I returned home that night, I went directly to the hiding place. I reached my hand in, much as one puts a finger in a coin-return slot, hoping to find something, yet knowing it's a hopeless gesture. There hadn't been any money in there for months. But yet, something had drawn me there. My hand touched a large envelope. In it was five thousand dollars!

Incredible? Yes. Impossible? Nothing is impossible with God.

The message was clear: *Put out, Joe! I'll provide, just like I say in My Word.*

Doors were opening for me more and more to hold meetings in prisons. On one occasion, the chaplain of a State correctional school invited me to speak to a large group of boys and girls fourteen to nineteen, some of whom had been imprisoned for murder. Thirty-five of these young people came to the altar to receive salvation.

At a follow-up counseling session, I learned that many of these young people who had been addicted to hard drugs such as heroin started out by taking tranquilizers or weight-reducing pills at an early age—some of them as young as eleven or twelve. When I asked them where they got the pills, many told of observing their mothers or fathers taking this medication. Curiosity got the best of them, and they stole pills from the medicine cabinets in their homes to see what the pills would do. They liked the "kick" or sensation, and so began the trail to addiction. Others of the kids had begun by sniffing glue.

I learned that ninety-nine percent of the young people in State schools are there directly or indirectly because of drugs. Seven out of ten young people try some form of drug before they reach the ninth grade.

One day after returning from a prison visit, I had a phone call from Jean, telling me that she had decided to move to California. My hopes shot up like a rocket! She *had* seen the change in me! My wishful thinking concluded that she was going to give our marriage another try. She promised that we'd see her within a few weeks, and from then on, the kids and I were floating on the clouds.

Then one night when I came home, Karen greeted me with the news that her mother was in town, staying with friends. She had visited the children that day.

I'd been kidding myself! Jean wasn't coming back to me. My wishful thinking had been without foundation, and I plunged from my dream world to earth's reality with a resounding thud.

Later, Jean found herself a place to live about fifteen miles from us. She went to work, but her weekends were free to spend with the kids. She still had no love for me, and I respectfully left her alone—but continued to pray.

In my ministry for Christ, I tried to cover as much territory as possible. I spent a great deal of time in my car and often saw hitchhikers on the road. I stopped for them whenever I got a specific nudge from the Holy Spirit.

One day I saw two pretty, barefoot girls on the off-ramp of the freeway, and I was led to park and walk back to talk to them. I learned that they were from New York and had hitchhiked for three thousand miles.

"Your parents are worried about you," I said. "And God loves you. He gave His only begotten Son, Jesus Christ, to die for your sins so you might be forgiven and receive eternal life."

It was a bold, abrupt speech, and I felt the Spirit of God—so strong! Both girls accepted Jesus on the spot and wept unashamedly. As soon as they were born again, I saw them healed of the bad colds and sore

145

throats they had been suffering from. They looked at me in awe as they wiped away their tears. As I left, I gave them some money and made them promise they would call their folks that night.

On another occasion, a twenty-year-old girl from Michigan and a young man of twenty-five were hitch-hiking, shouldering the huge packs hikers often carry. They looked so weary, I was led to stop my car. They were a congenial, friendly pair, and I promised to drive them to the home of a pal some seven miles away.

As soon as they were in my car, I started telling them about my past life, how I'd made thousands of dollars a week a little more than a year ago, but was always desperately lonely, always searching—seeking the way to true happiness. I mentioned being at gatherings with politicians, gangsters, and movie people who were also empty and lonely and looking for a solution to their problems....

"You know, kids," I told them, "if anyone had told me two years ago that I'd be preaching Jesus, I'd have said they were crazy. I didn't believe in God or Christ. I thought Christians were weak, sick people who needed something to lean on. But I met Jesus in my bedroom one morning without anyone preaching to me or teaching me."

We talked about Christ, and I told them of the vision I'd had of His face. Then we pulled over under a large shade tree and they asked Him to take away their sins and come into their hearts and lives as their Savior. As they ended their prayer, I could see the tears welling in their eyes.

Then they told me that just an hour before I'd given them a lift, they had been picked up by a van of Jesus People who had told the couple of God's love for them.

The Lord said that some would plant the seeds and some would water them, but God Himself would reap the harvest. I am overjoyed to be involved in any stage of the process.

146

Early in July, I had a call from Bud Suhl, a man who had appeared on one of our TV broadcasts. Bud had been a high liver, wheeling and dealing in stocks and bank transactions as well as in people's lives. Gambling had been his downfall. At the peak of his habit, he was betting as much as ten thousand dollars a day! After a losing streak, he came up short about a million dollars on his books and was sentenced to thirty years in prison.

While serving his time, Bud attended a service in the prison chapel and asked Jesus to come into his heart. From that day, his whole life underwent a dramatic change. Within fourteen months, Bud was paroled, his new life dedicated to spreading the Good News about Jesus.

Bud runs a plant in Glendale, California, where he hires many ex-convicts. All the profits go into buying Bibles and religious literature for prisoners and the poor. Every morning between nine and ten, a Bible study is held at his factory. Even the switchboard operator is in on it, greeting every incoming call with, "Good day—and God bless you!"

Bud asked me if I'd like to go to Mexico with him to visit churches and missionaries and a penal institution for boys. When I said yes, he tried to warn me. "Everyone else who has gone there with me has broken down and wept." But his warning didn't begin to prepare me for what I was to experience there.

The boys' prison was located below Mexicali, about a six-hour drive from home. Bud had gathered a large truckload of used clothing, food, Bibles and other supplies for them and for some church missions in Mexico. His wife Shirley, and Pauline, a black girl who loves Jesus, spent much of the night before our trip frying chicken to feed the more than 120 boys in the jail. There were also packages of candy in the truck for them.

I was at Bud's house at 4:00 A.M., and we set off. With us were Ray, who had spent twenty years in prison,

Bud's eight-year-old son, an older neighbor boy, Bud's wife, and Pauline. I drove Bud's station wagon, following the truck.

The refrigeration unit in the truck was broken, and soon after sunrise, the temperature reached the nineties. We prayed that God would keep the fried chicken from spoiling. When we arrived at the Mexican border, the temperature was well over 100, and the air was very humid and sticky. We bought forty gallons of ice cold milk there, knowing we were not far from our destination.

There were lines of trucks waiting for clearance at the border, but God was with us, and we were cleared within thirty minutes.

We drove the last five miles to the boys' jail over an unpaved dirt road. Because of the dust barrage kicked up by the truck, I couldn't see twenty feet ahead of me. Even with the windows closed, the dust sifted through cracks and filled the car. We arrived sweating profusely, covered with dirt and grime.

A civilian met us at the front gate which was set in a high fence with rolls of barbed wire on top of it. I couldn't believe that all that was for young kids!

As we drove into the compound, the boys were lining up. "It's chow time," Ray explained. "We're just in time."

There were about 120 boys from the ages of six to seventeen. Many had no shirts; most had no shoes. But what got to me was the hurt and sorrow in their eyes. It pierced to the marrow of my soul.

The boys helped us unload the chicken, milk, and other things, and carry them into the cafeteria. The food was still cold though the outside temperature was now 110 degrees. God had heard our prayers and kept the food from spoiling.

The cafeteria was a big dark room permeated with the stench of sewer gas. I looked around at the crude tables, the battered old benches, the torn window-screens, and I shook my head in disbelief. The meal already prepared for the boys was a large pan of rice, a pot of watery soup, some greasy-looking beans, and a big box of stale rolls. For dessert, there were speckled oranges and bruised apples, fruit much too deteriorated to be sold in a market. Everything was crawling with flies.

The unappetizing food was piled onto dented tin trays, and the only eating implements were rust-pitted enamel spoons that had long since lost most of their enamel.

"O God," my heart cried, "I'll never complain about anything again." I fought back the tears for these little guys, living in a hell on earth. I was thankful that for this meal, the boys would have all the fried chicken they could eat and fresh, clean milk to drink. How good it would taste to them.

When the boys were all seated at three large benches, we began to tell them of God's love for them. But I wondered how they could believe that God loved them when He permitted them to live in such sordid surroundings.

Each of us gave our testimony. Bud and Ray were able to speak to the boys in Spanish, and Bud translated for me as I invited the boys to accept Jesus as their Savior. About sixty of them repeated the sinner's prayer with me.

Afterward, while the boys were finishing their meal, I slipped outside and walked around aimlessly, tears streaming down my face at the awful degradation, the hopelessness of the place. After a while, Ray came out and joined me. Aware of the agony I was going through, he patted me on the back, his own eyes brimming.

"It's okay, Joe," he said, trying to console me. "I've been here before, and I'm still not used to it."

The man in charge allowed us to visit one of the sleeping quarters, a cinderblock building with a door of three-inch-thick steel. The only ventilation came from a few six-inch slits ten feet above the cement floor. Each bunk

149

held a thin mattress, disintegrating with filth, and a ragged blanket. There were no sheets, no toilets, no washbowls, and the stench was sickening. We learned that the buildings were not heated, even though the winters got as bitter cold as the summers got broiling hot.

The look on the faces of the boys as we left that day almost wrenched my heart out of me. Riding along in the truck, full of unendurable anguish over the wretchedness I'd just seen, I turned it over and over in my mind. I knew the Lord had brought me there for a reason. But what was it? Were we to establish a school for these boys? Surely the authorities would be glad to wash their hands of them. My thoughts churned, but no answer came.

Our next stop was a little village Bud had visited before. Kids popped out from everywhere, barefooted, dirty, beautiful, happy little urchins, glad to see us, reaching out eagerly for the cans of dried malted milk Bud had brought them. Most of their houses were without electricity or heat, and all water had to be carried from a creek which was a sickly dark green color. But all the kids looked healthy—and happy. Physical poverty didn't have to mean a lack of joy in people's lives, I knew that. Spiritual poverty was the thing that hurt. Again I saw the haunting eyes of the boys at the prison.

Leaving the village, we drove for quite a distance to a newly constructed one-room building, the "Jesus Saves Church." It was about twice the size of a garage, and the crude wooden benches were upholstered with multicolored scraps of carpeting. Bud knew the congregation well, and he had brought them clothes, food, and Bibles.

The pastor's wife opened the evening prayer service with a prayer (her husband was working late that day), and the village children sang some hymns about Jesus. Bud interpreted while I spoke, then he preached a sermon. We were richly blessed by the sweet spirit of the God-loving people.

Our next stop was a small brick church on another dusty road in another village where most of the houses had been put together from scraps of large wooden and cardboard cartons. The two missionaries themselves, a happy eighty-three-years-young Mrs. Austin and her middle-aged daughter, lived in a twenty-foot trailer with electricity but no indoor plumbing. A large barrel with a lid on it held their water supply, carried in buckets from a creek about a block away.

The village people had helped them build a brick church, and everyone had contributed his share of hard work, sweat, and faith. No wonder they were so proud of their project.

As we unloaded food and clothing, we made notes of additional needed supplies and Bud promised to bring them the next time he came. Mrs Austin's sewing machine, the only one in the village, the one on which she had made clothes for the village children, had a burned-out motor. God would provide a replacement within a few weeks.

Though cramped in their small trailer, the missionaries never complained, but thanked God for the privilege of serving Him in Mexico.

We hadn't been there long when children began to gather, all clean and sparkling, ready for their Bible study. It was easy to see that they loved their little church.

As we left the missionaries, God laid His hand on my heart, and I took most of the cash from my pocket and left it with them for God's work in that place. Dirty and worn out as I was, I felt a shower of spiritual refreshment wash over me, after obeying the Spirit of the Lord.

Winding down more dusty roads, we visited other small congregations, in other inelegant buildings that, to the villagers, were as grand as Notre Dame Cathedral. Everywhere we went, we left clothing and supplies, and came away enriched by the appreciation and prayers of God's people.

Finally, after a late prayer meeting under a night sky filled with stars, we headed for our last stop, Pablo's house, in Mexicali.

Pablo was a thirty-year-old Mexican who had met Jesus as his Savior in prison. God led him to study the Bible, and then He opened the doors for Pablo to preach in the boys' prisons in the surrounding area. Pablo walked the dusty roads for miles, carrying books and Bibles for the young people. When we had unloaded our gifts of Bibles and clothing from the truck, Pablo's wife produced a large bottle of warm soda pop which we gratefully shared with one another. Then Pablo shared his dream of building a small church next-door to his modest home. Together, we prayed that God would bring it to pass.

Then Pablo's family joined us in praying that we'd be given strength and protection for our trip home. We would need it. We had a five-hour drive ahead of us, and it was already midnight. It had been a long day.

After an hour of driving, all of us realized we were too exhausted to drive safely, and so we pulled off the road at a rest area, trusting a brief nap would revive us. As I lay there, stretched out on a large picnic table, gazing up at the heavens, I prayed. "God, You've done so much. Will You give those poor boys in that prison some decent facilities? Will You help me to help them?"

Galaxies of billions of stars twinkled above me, too many for man to count, but I knew that every single one of them had been put precisely into its own special, unique place by a Creator whose very nature is love. I had asked Him only to take care of a handful of Mexican boys, and somehow, suddenly, I was satisfied. I knew He would do it.

While I was away from home, Jean was seeing more and more of our children. I was trusting that this would soften her heart toward the possibility of our family being reunited. I agreed that the children should go on a vacation with her to Utah. As I took the three of them to the airport, I tried once again to tell Jean that Jesus could heal all those years of misery I had caused her—if only she'd let Him. She listened quietly, but said nothing.

While they were gone, I prayed constantly that the Lord would work a miracle, but when they returned in August, nothing had changed. As far as Jean was concerned, she had found a new life with love, peace, and security—and the kids. Indeed, she had a right to all that after what she'd suffered during my violent past. Nonetheless, I kept hoping and praying for a miracle in which Jean would be reborn and we could spend a beautiful life on earth together serving God and then spend eternity in heaven. That was the way it ended in the movies, but in real life I was learning there are often times when a Christian is called to reap what he has sown. And I am learning to rejoice in whatever God plans for my life.

In the meantime, I have not forgotten the charge that God gave me when He said, *Tell your friends.*

I haven't yet had many opportunities for direct confrontation with my friends who were still active in the underworld, and I was praying about this recently.

"Lord, You said, 'Tell your friends,' but You're going to have to open the doors for me. I don't have the muscle or the entree that I used to have."

As I was praying, it came to me that maybe He *had* opened some doors, and that I was soon to learn about them.

The next afternoon I got a call at 2:00 sharp, which seems to be a favorite time for the Holy Spirit to cause things to happen in my life.

"Hello, Reverend?"

"Yes?" I couldn't recognize the gravelly voice or the heavy Italian dialect, and I wondered if it might be one of my friends playing a joke.

153

"You don't mind if I call you Reverend?"

"No, I don't mind," and I started to laugh, in spite of myself. "Who is this?"

And he told me. Cigaro! I laughed harder.

"Oh, you're laughing? It's funny?"

"No, no, I'm glad you called. Say, how you been, anyway?"

"Oh, fine, Joey, just fine. I been hearing about your religion, and I just wondered how things were going."

"Pretty good."

"Listen, Reverend—you don't mind if I call you Reverend?"

"No," I gasped between half-swallowed bursts of laughter. "Not at all."

"You know, I might go in the same racket you're in."

And I completely broke up, because I knew he was serious. And then I told him briefly what had happened to me on March 8, 1972. He listened politely, then said, "Oh, it happened in 1972, eh? Well, I might get, how you say, 'saved.' Joey, I gonna call you about that sometime."

It got real silent then for a moment. He didn't want to hang up and neither did I. "Hey, I was talking to a Christian friend of mine in the FBI. He tells me they're looking at you and (here I named another biggie in the family) and they're expecting a little war between you two."

"Oh," he said, trying to mask his real interest. "When he tell you that, Joey?"

"A few weeks ago. And they're starting to pick up the bodies."

"What did you tell him, Joey?" he asked slowly.

"I told him that God had told me to tell you about Jesus!"

"You told him right, Joey," he said, noticeably relieved. "You told him right."

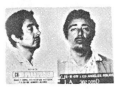

STATE OF CALIFORNIA
DEPARTMENT OF JUSTICE
BUREAU OF IDENTIFICATION
P O Box 1859, Sacramento

CII 1111107

BLK BLU 5-7 145 Pa. 8-8-30

JOSEPH DONATO

FORM C-11 8A

IS FOR OFFICIAL USE ONLY

FBI 5 147 923

DL# J 827232

ALIAS: JOSEPH D. DONATO, JOSEPH DAVID DONATO,
JOSEPH DANIEL DONATO:

ARRESTED OR RECEIVED	DEPARTMENT AND NUMBER	NAME	CHARGE	DISPOSITION
9-22-47	PD READING, PA. 3692	JOSEPH DONATO	BURG.	TOT PROB. OFF.
6-20-48	BERKS CO. PR. READING, PA. 385-48	JOSEPH DONATO	WATKINS FIREARMS ACT	
5-12-52	PD HAWTHORNE NAA 999	JOSEPH DONATO	APPLICANT	
12-13-54	BERKS CO. PR. READING, PA. 385-48	JOSEPH DONATO	A&B & SURETY OF THE PEACE; SURETY OF THE PEACE(2 cts) AGGRAVATED A&B	12-13-54 DISCH. ON BAIL
3-7-57	PD LOS ANGELES 382089-D	JOSEPH DONATO	SUSP. BKMKG.	
9-16-57	PD LOS ANGELES 382089-D	JOSEPH DONATO	23.23 MC	9-30-57, NG
1 24 58	PD LOS ANGELES 382089-D	JOSEPH D. DONATO	SUSP. BOOKIE	1-29-58, Rel.
5-3-60	ST.DEPT.ALCOHOLIC BEVERAGE CONTROL LOS ANGLES,136434	JOSEPH DONATO	APPLICANT	NO LONGER LICENSED
6-1-61	PD LOS ANGELES 382089-D	JOSEPH DANIEL DONATO	BKMKG. FEL. HTA: 3 cts 337A PC	6-4-62,SENT 90 DS. CO. JAIL; SUS. PROB. 3YRS:PAY FINE OF$250. PLUS PA ON CT 1&3; CT2 NG.
6-1-61	COUNTY PROB. DEPT LOS ANGELES, X-231043	JOSEPH D. DONATO	337a PC CTS. 1&3	6-4-62,90 DS. CJ. SS, 3 YRS. PROB. 6 3 63, BKI.
11-17-61	PD BURBANK, ID#50461	JOSEPH DONATO	SUSPR.MURDER 836.3 PC	
11-20-61	SO LOS ANGELES B-815669	JOSEPH D DONATO	MURDER	1-30-63, NT. GLTY.
11-3-64	PD BURBANK 50461	JOSEPH DAVID DONATO	ASLT. W/INT. TU COMM. MURDER	COMPL.REFUSES TO PROSEC.
8-30-68	SO SAN DIEGO 334684	JOSEPH DONATO	CONSPIRACY, BURG.	
4-30-69	PD LOS ANGELES 382089-D/118468	JOSEPH DANIEL DONATO	337a PC BKMKG	
5-8-69	PD LOS ANGELES 382089-D/124202	JOSEPH DANILE DONATO	487.1 PC GT	
6-13-69	PD LOS ANGELES 382089-D/148842	JOSEPH DANIEL DONATO	WARR. 487,PC. 1 CT 337a PC	12-16-69,"A" DISM. FOJ (NO FURTH.INFO

*Those wishing to participate in
Joe Donato's ministry may reach
the author at the following address.*

Joseph Donato
P.O. BOX 16373
FRESNO, CA 93755

SOME ANSWERS

This is the eigth printing of this book - in the year 2000.

I've traveled 3,000,000 miles and lived in South Africa for four years.

I have traveled from Europe, to India, Africa to Canada, the Far East to Mexico, and across the U.S. sharing my life story with millions of people, through the media, plus magazines and newspapers.

In one years time this speaker has logged 100,000 miles.

Much of our mail asks, "What happened to Jean?" She remarried someone else 3½ years later.

My children are doing fine and are very close to me.

Rudy, Bob, and Boom Boom had the same miracle that I experienced.

Cigaro died 3 years later in San Diego, in a hail of an assassin's bullets.

If you wish to contact me, Write

Joseph Donato

P.O. BOX 16373
FRESNO, CA 93755